"Do we worship the same God? This is such an important question today. These groundbreaking high-quality essays from Christians, Jews, and a Muslim open important doors onto new paths."

— **Gavin D'Costa**
University of Bristol

"None of the contributors to this collection gives a clear, simple answer to the question that perplexes them all. And that's what makes this conversation so engaging and enlightening. Each of the authors responds with a 'yes but no' or a 'no but yes.' Together, they draw on tradition, philosophy, scriptural analysis, and — especially — mysticism to affirm both the depth and the diversity of faiths that call themselves monotheistic."

— **Paul F. Knitter**
Union Theological Seminary

"This extremely noteworthy book deals with a very critical and thorny issue, which is most often avoided. Highly academic and intellectually stimulating, this is also one of the most hopeful texts I have read on this subject. It is of critical significance for anyone involved in theologies of religion, especially within the 'monotheistic' or 'Abrahamic' tradition. . . . Imperative for anybody involved in interfaith dialogue."

— **Charles Amjad-Ali**
Luther Seminary

Do We Worship the Same God?

JEWS, CHRISTIANS, AND MUSLIMS IN DIALOGUE

Edited by

Miroslav Volf

WILLIAM B. EERDMANS PUBLISHING COMPANY

GRAND RAPIDS, MICHIGAN / CAMBRIDGE, U.K.

Published 2012 by

Wm. B. Eerdmans Publishing Co.

2140 Oak Industrial Drive N.E., Grand Rapids, Michigan 49505 /

P.O. Box 163, Cambridge CB3 9PU U.K.

Printed in the United States of America

17 16   7 6 5 4 3

Library of Congress Cataloging-in-Publication Data

Do we worship the same God?: Jews, Christians, and Muslims in dialogue /
    edited by Miroslav Volf.
        p.   cm.
    ISBN 978-0-8028-6689-9 (pbk.: alk. paper)
    1. God. 2. Abrahamic religions. 3. Religions — Relations. 4. Judaism.
    5. Christianity. 6. Islam.   I. Volf, Miroslav.

    BL473.D6   2012
    201′.5 — dc23

                                                        2012009877

www.eerdmans.com

Contents

v

Introduction

Ever since 9/11 the question whether Muslims and Christians worship the same God has persistently followed me wherever I go speaking about relations between these two religions. Muslims don't push the question. Christians do, vigorously — in Europe, Asia, and Africa no less than in North America. Maybe that's not surprising. The terrorists who flew the planes on that suicidal mission were instructed in their manual: "Remember, this is a battle for the sake of God." In the name of God and with expectations of glory in this world and rewards in the next, they killed themselves and thousands of innocent civilians. To many Christians it seems obvious that the God who spills the blood of the innocent and rewards suicidal missions with paradisiacal pleasures can't be the God they worship. What many Christians aren't aware of is that that may be obvious to many Muslims as well.

But the question isn't mainly about the terrorists and their God. It's about Muslims generally. It draws its energy from a deep concern. To ask: "Do we have a common God?" is, among other things, to worry: "Can we live together?" That's why whether or not a given community worships the same god as does another community has always been a crucial cultural and political question and not just a theological one.

Live together Muslims and Christians will!

- Christianity and Islam are today the most numerous and fastest growing religions globally. Together they encompass more than half of humanity. *Consequence:* both are here to stay.

- As a result of globalization, ours is an interconnected and interdependent world. Religions are intermingled within single states and across their boundaries. *Consequence:* Muslims and Christians will increasingly share common spaces.
- Since both religions are by their very nature "socially engaged" — they are world-transforming religions of a prophetic type — and since their followers mostly embrace democratic ideals, they will continue to push for their vision of the good life in the public square. *Consequence:* tensions, even conflicts between Muslims and Christians, are unavoidable.

Growing, intertwined, and assertive — communities of Muslims and Christians will live together.

Muslims and Christians can work together to depose dictators and assert the power of the people; we've seen it happen in the Tahrir Square in Cairo during the 2011 revolution in Egypt, with devout Muslims and Coptic Christians protesting side by side. But can Muslims and Christians also work together to build a flourishing democratic society in which rights of all would be respected, the rights of minority Coptic Christians no less than the rights of majority Muslims? They can, if they have a common set of fundamental values. But do they? Only if Muslims and Christians, both monotheists committed to seeing in the attributes of God their fundamental values, have a common God. But do they?

At the height of the Iraq War in 2004, influential TV evangelist and former U.S. presidential candidate Pat Robertson said: "The entire world is being convulsed by a religious struggle. The fight is not about money or territory; it is not about poverty versus wealth; it is not about ancient customs versus modernity. No. The struggle is whether Hubal, the Moon God of Mecca, known as Allah, is supreme, or whether the Judeo-Christian Jehovah God of the Bible is supreme." That was a war cry! God vs. Allah.

The dispute is not about the divine name, "God" or "Allah," as some ignorantly claim. Arab Christians have for centuries worshiped God under the name "Allah"; the Copts in Egypt, a persecuted minority, use "Allah" to refer to the God of Jesus Christ who is the Holy Trinity. The dispute is about the divine identity: Do Muslims and Christians pray to two different deities so that, given that both are strict monotheists, one group prays to a false god and are therefore idolaters whereas the other prays to a true God?

Many Christians through the centuries, saints and undisputed great teachers, have believed that Muslims worship the same God as they do —

the same God, though differently understood, of course. They did so even in times of Muslim cultural ascendency, military conquests, and grave threat to Christianity in the whole of Europe. After the fall of Constantinople (1453), the city named after the first Christian emperor and a seat of Christendom for over 1,000 years, Cardinal Nicholas of Cusa, a towering intellect and an experienced church diplomat, affirmed unambiguously that Muslims and Christians worship the same God, albeit in part differently understood.

But was the learned cardinal from centuries past right? Or might the popular TV evangelist have been closer to the truth, notwithstanding the exaggerated character of the contrast he drew? The issue continues to be hotly debated. Under the auspices of the "God and Human Flourishing Program" housed in the Yale Center for Faith and Culture (www.yale.edu/faith), my two colleagues (David Kelsey and John Hare) and I have organized two consultations about the question. Selected papers from these two consultations are printed in this book.

To the first consultation we invited only Christian theologians. Since little had been written on the topic at that time, we as Christians had to sort things for ourselves — get clarity not just about what the position might be but even more fundamentally about how we might go about determining our position. The essays by Amy Plantinga Pauw (Louisville Presbyterian Seminary), Christoph Schöbel (University of Tübingen, and Denys Turner (Yale University) were presented at that consultation.

To the second consultation we invited Jewish and Muslim scholars as well. Jews, Muslims, and Christians have traditionally each had their own views on whether the other two communities worship the same God as they do. For instance, Christians have always believed that they worshiped the same God as the Jews even though Christians think of Jesus Christ as God incarnate and hold that the One God is the Holy Trinity, whereas the Jews contest these claims. For Christians believe that they worship the God of Abraham and Sarah, the God of Moses and Isaiah, the God of the Jews. For the most part, Jews do not think that they worship the same God as Christians do; on account of Christian worship of Jesus Christ, they deem Christians to be idolaters and therefore not true monotheists. Each community also has its own modes of reflection about the issue. Still, notwithstanding the fact that each Abrahamic faith community — Jews, Christians, and Muslims — has its own specific perspective on the issue, theologians from each community should take into account arguments of the other two. Hence, though the focus of the second consultation was on the Christian perspectives on whether Muslims and Christians have a common God, we needed to listen to perspectives of Jewish and Muslim religious thinkers and to let them look over our shoulders as we tried to craft our own position. The texts by Alon Goshen-Gottstein (Elijah Institute, Israel), Reza Shah-Kazemi (Institute of Ismaili Studies, London), and Peter Ochs (University of Virginia) fulfill that function.

Some of the intellectually most stimulating discussions that I have ever engaged in happened in the course of these two consultations. The discussions touched on matters of ultimate concern (and highest complexity), they concerned relations among the three monotheistic faiths, and they were carried against the backdrop of mutual enmity and violence, of conflicts with a centuries-long history that continue still today. The papers and discussions stimulated my own work on the topic, which was published as *Allah: A Christian Response* (HarperOne, 2011). I hope that the essays, now collected in this book, will stimulate broad and deep reflections and discussions on this issue of singular religious, cultural, and political importance.

T. J. Dumansky took the lion's share of the responsibility of organizing the consultations and, together with Jan O'Dell, my assistant at the Yale Center for Faith and Culture, helped host them at the Yale Divinity School. Christopher Corbin helped with editing the texts for publication. Jon Pott and his staff at Eerdmans made them into a book. To them all I am very grateful. My deepest thanks goes to Alonzo McDonald and his Agape Foundation, which financed the consultations as well as the editing. But the most extraordinary thing about Alonzo McDonald was that he, an octogenarian with no training in theology or religious studies, was an active and constructive participant in these discussions.

Miroslav Volf

The Same God? The Perspective of Faith, the Identity of God, Tolerance, and Dialogue

Christoph Schwöbel

Who's to Decide?

The question whether Judaism, Christianity, and Islam worship and believe in the same God is an intensely debated issue of theological reflection in each of the three traditions and one of the central topics of conversations between the three monotheistic religions often grouped together as the Abrahamic faiths. The declaration of the Second Vatican Council, *Nostra Aetate,* is often referred to as indicating that Christians and Muslims worship the same God. On closer inspection, however, a different and more complicated picture emerges. *Nostra Aetate* emphasizes that all peoples are one community *(una communitas),* have one origin, since God let the whole of humankind live on earth *(unam habent originem cum Deus omne genus hominum inhabitare fecerit super universam faciem terrae),* and have one ultimate goal *(unum etiam habent finem ultimum, Deum . . .).* It also underlines that the various religions expect an answer to the riddles of the human condition, which culminate in the question of the ultimate and ineffable mystery of our existence, from which we have our beginning and toward which we strive *(quid demum illud ultimum et ineffabile mysterium quod nostram existentiam amplectitur, ex quo ortum sumimus et quo tendimus).* This, however, is not primarily an anthropological constant, an essential feature of the human condition; rather it is rooted in the fact that God's providence and the testimony of his goodness as well as God's counsel of salvation extend to all peoples. There is a carefully balanced tension in these statements between emphasizing God as the one universal origin and goal of the whole of humankind, and at the same time stressing that the elect will be united in the Holy City, which will be illumined by the glory of God. The universality of the common origin and common goal is balanced by the emphasis on God's election, which, again, is balanced by stressing that all peoples will walk in the light of God's glory.

It is this theological framework that in *Nostra Aetate* provides the background for the anthropological statement that humans expect from the religions — a response to the recondite enigmas of the human condition, even an answer to the ultimate mystery of the origin and goal of our existence. How is that to be understood epistemologically? Do the religions know that the origin and goal of all peoples are one and the same God? *Nostra Aetate* offers a complex and highly differentiated answer to the question: the same God? First of all, it is stated that from the earliest times until today there is in all the diverse peoples some sort of perception *(quaedam perceptio)* of the hidden power that is present to the course of events in the world and to the events of human life. Sometimes there is even a certain recognition or acknowledgment *(aliquando agnitio)* of a highest Godhead, or even of a Father *(Summi Numinis vel etiam Patris)*. This *perceptio* or even *agnitio* penetrates the life of the diverse peoples with an intimate religious sense *(intimo sensu religioso)*. This is the reason why the religions strive to respond in subtle concepts and by means of a highly developed language to respond to the same questions *(ad easdem quaestiones respondere satagunt)*. As far as I can see, this is the only explicit identity claim that is made in *Nostra Aetate*. Do we have to conclude that *Nostra Aetate* avoids claiming that the religions worship the same God while explicitly stating that they attempt to provide an answer to the same question concerning human existence, a question that is rooted in their perception and even recognition of a divine power?

Nostra Aetate presents the religions in a perspective of concentric circles, a method also used in other documents of Vatican II, starting from the outer circles and proceeding to the inner circles. In Hinduism people scrutinize the divine mystery *(homines mysterium divinum scrutantur)* and express it in the form of mythologies, philosophical reflections, ascetic lifestyles, and meditation. Seeking refuge in God with love and confidence is also seen as one of the expressions of this scrutiny of the divine mystery. In Buddhism, recognition of the radical insufficiency of the mutable world leads to teaching a way that people can attain perfect liberation or the highest illumination. It should be noted that *Nostra Aetate* does not claim that this is what Buddhists and Hindus seek, do, or strive for, but that it is what people in Hinduism and Buddhism attempt to attain. It is, it seems, not a statement of what Hindus and Buddhists of the various sects would describe as their self-understanding; rather, it is a description from the perspective of Catholic Christian faith, based on the notion that all humans expect from the religions answers to the riddles of the human condition and the mystery of our existence. With regard to other religions mentioned generally in the same circle, it is simply said that they strive to meet the restlessness of the human heart (Augustine's famous metaphor) in various ways: by teaching, precepts for living, and holy rites.

The summary statement is again finely balanced: the Catholic Church does not reject anything in these religions that is true and holy *(nihil eorum, quae in his religionibus vera et sancta sunt)*. It considers with sincere attention *(sincera observantia)* the modes of action and living and the precepts and doctrines that these religions represent. The reason for this attitude is that they often *(haud raro)* emit a ray of that truth which illumines all humans, although the teachings of these religions show in many ways discrepancies from what the Catholic Church itself holds and proposes. If we try to unpack this statement we have to say that the Catholic Church does not reject anything that is true and holy in the religions because it recognizes that what is true and holy in them refers to the Truth, which illumines all people. We find here a referential criterion for assessing what is true and holy in other religions. Although there are many discrepancies in the doctrines, precepts, et cetera of the religions from what the Catholic Church itself teaches, it recognizes nevertheless a ray of the truth that illumines all humans. The basis for this view is the common origin and goal of all humankind in God, which lets all people strive for an answer to the mystery of human existence, the perception and even recognition of this hidden divine power in the religions, and the eschatological expectation that in the end, when the elect will be united in the Holy City — which is illumined by the Glory of God — all people will walk in the light of this glory.

However, in addition to a basis for such a referential view we need a criterion to assess what refers to the truth and in what way it refers to it. The criterion offered in *Nostra Aetate* is Christological: The Catholic Church proclaims Christ who is "the way, the truth, and the life," in whom people find the fullness of religious life and in whom God has reconciled the world with himself. This seems to suggest that the fullness of truth can

3

be found in Christ as well as the way by means of which we can attain it. While the referential basis makes sure that all religions can refer to the one divine truth, the referential criterion allows the Catholic Church to ascertain to what extent they refer to the one truth. This is the basis for the exhortation to all Catholics for conversation and cooperation with the religions as well as for recognizing, preserving, and promoting the spiritual and moral goods and the sociocultural values they find in them by witnessing to Christ in faith and in life.

This is *prima facie* a somewhat bewildering statement. However, if Christ is the criterion of truth and therefore the content of Christian witness, Christ is also the criterion for recognizing, preserving, and promoting spiritual and moral good, as well as sociocultural values Catholics find in other religions.

When we now turn to what *Nostra Aetate* says about Muslims we find a number of remarkable changes in comparison to the treatment of Hinduism and Buddhism. *Nostra Aetate* does not state what people do in Islam as it states what people do in Hinduism or Buddhism, but says that Muslims adore the only God, the living and subsisting, the merciful and omnipotent creator of heaven and earth who has spoken to humans *(unicum Deum adorant, viventem et subsistentem, misericordem et omnipotentem, Creatorem caeli et terrae, homines allocutum)*. This statement is supported by a reference to Gregory VII's letter to Al-Nasir, King of Mauritania, which also asserts that Muslims and Christians believe and confess one God, "albeit in different ways." The interesting feature here is that the text emphasizes the points of referential convergence between the Christian understanding of God and the Muslim understanding of God, but does so in a way that gives precedence to what Muslims would stress in their understanding of God, the singularity and unity of God, that God is living and self-subsistent, merciful, and omnipotent, that God is creator of heaven and earth and has spoken to humans. What we see here is reference by definite description, offering descriptions on which Christians and Muslims agree. These descriptions specify Muslim *worship*. This seems particularly apt because acts of worship are shaped by the object of worship and have the same referential logic, which seems to be applied throughout *Nostra Aetate*. With regard to the first statement of the treatment of Islam in section 3, we can say that referential convergence establishes propositional consensus.

In what follows, this referential logic is applied to central aspects of Islamic faith. In this way *Nostra Aetate* states that Muslims try hard to submit with all their soul to the hidden counsels of God, just as Abraham submitted himself to God, Abraham to whom Muslim faith likes to refer. By referring to submission to God — to Islam in other words — *Nostra Aetate* can take up Muslim self-understanding by seeing it exemplified in Abraham to whom both Christians and Muslims (and of course first and foremost, Jews) refer. This reference to Abraham, however, leaves it open that Christians and Muslims refer to Abraham in different ways, although both see him as exemplary for the human relationship to God.

When *Nostra Aetate* mentions Jesus and Mary, the document explicitly states the differences between Muslim and Catholic views with regard to Jesus and implicitly with regard to Mary. Concerning Jesus it says that he is venerated as a prophet by Muslims but not acknowledged as God (*quidem ut Deum non agnoscunt*), and that also marks a decisive difference in the view of Mary, although Muslims can invoke Mary in prayer, which Protestants, for instance, would hesitate to do. The expectation of the Last Judgment and of resurrection of the dead is also mentioned — so it seems — as a point of agreement. The last element of the description of Islamic religion mentions prayer, almsgiving, and fasting.

It is quite clear that this is a description of Islam from a Christian perspective, which interprets Islam as a form of believing in the one God on the basis of the criteria of Christian faith, what we have called the referential basis and the referential criterion. By focusing on the points of convergence in understanding God as the object of reference of Christian and Muslim faith, it is therefore suggested that Muslims and Christians worship the one and only God, however differently. This difference in Muslim worship and belief is, from a Christian perspective, a deficiency. However, if one concentrates on that which would suggest a "referential identity" in Muslim and Christian faith in God, as it is expressed from a Christian perspective, this also implies — from a Muslim point of view — that the description of Islam is deficient. It mentions neither Muhammad nor the *Hadj*. Referential convergence or identity, i.e., convergence or identity with regard to the referent, does not exclude deficient description — for either of the two perspectives. However, it is clear that the Council does not expect the religions to meet on the basis of their respective deficiencies as they are perceived from either side, but on the basis of those shared elements that lead to the perception of deficiencies.

If we look at the conclusion of the paragraph on Islam it is clear that what has been stated is in the view of the Council sufficient to offer an exhortation to "all" *(omnes)*, in view of the dissent and inimical relations between Muslims and Christians in history, to leave the past aside, to work for mutual understanding *(ad comprehensionem mutuam)* and protect and promote together *(communiter)* social justice and moral goods, not least, peace and freedom for the whole of humankind. The wording seems to suggest that what has been mentioned as a convergence in Christian and Muslim faith is sufficient to call for mutual understanding and communal engagement for justice, moral goods, peace, and freedom. This is presented as a step into the future, leaving aside the struggles of the past. One could say that *Nostra Aetate* does not so much seek to establish a common dogmatic ground between Catholic Christian faith and Muslim faith but common ethical aims. However, there is sufficient common ground, the alleged commonality of referring to the one and only God, to address both sides *(omnes)* with the exhortation to exercise *mutual* comprehension and strive together *(communiter)* for common goals.

Does *Nostra Aetate* state that Christians and Muslims worship and believe in the same God? I think one could only say that *Nostra Aetate* states that Christians and Muslims worship the one and only God because there is only one God who is the origin and goal of the whole of humankind. There is thus an identity of reference, more precisely an identity of the referent (the object of reference) in the way Christians and Muslims understand God. According to *Nostra Aetate* this can be known from the perspective of the Catholic Church on the basis of the Christian understanding of God, which defines the epistemic perspective from which the relationship to the religions is assessed. This identity of reference establishes a convergence of definite descriptions about the referent. This convergence, however, implies and requires only a partial consensus of descriptions. While part of the descriptions can be formulated in a partial propositional consensus, there is also a partial dissensus, and for each of the perspectives this makes the other perspective deficient. This deficiency, however, does not preclude the possibility, indeed, the need of mutual comprehension or the shared striving for common aims.

The apparent modesty of the claims suggested by *Nostra Aetate* points to the central issue of the question whether Christians and Muslims worship and believe in the same God. Who is to decide? The question seems to suggest that there could be a position *above* the different religious perspectives of the two religions. It seems to me that, at least until the *visio beatifica*, there is no such perspective. There is no view from nowhere. If there were, it would be irrelevant to the question because any answer that is not an answer given by Muslims or Christians is quite irrelevant, since it could not help to shape the relationship between Muslims and Christians. Their mutual relationship can be shaped by Christians or Muslims only on the basis of grounds that are particular to their respective perspectives of faith.

One can also offer strong epistemological grounds that every kind of knowledge is bound to a particular perspective and must start from there. This is at least true, if we want to act on that knowledge. It is usually accepted that finite agents must act from somewhere, from a particular standpoint of action. What is accepted as unproblematic with regard to action applies in the same way to knowledge — at least if it is the kind of knowledge on the basis of which we are prepared to act. Therefore there can be no abstract criteria of "sameness" that could function apart from any particular epistemic perspective. Even logical criteria of sameness have to be applied from some perspective to a particular problem as it appears from that perspective. The grounds that can be offered for either stating sameness or difference will therefore depend on the way they appear from a particular perspective.

The obvious objection to this emphasis on the epistemic significance of perspectives for any kind of knowledge is that it leads to a kind of relativistic perspectivism, which is often associated with Friedrich Nietzsche. This perspectivism takes its most radical form if it is suggested that each perspective constitutes incommensurable ways of looking at reality or even expresses different realities. If that were the case, it would neither be possible to state from a particular perspective a universal truth claim nor to contest what is claimed from one perspective to another. The latter is of course the demise of all truth claims, because propositions can only claim truth if their negation is wrong. This kind of relativistic perspectivism is the end of all communication, which depends on the law of noncontradiction that p and not-p cannot have the same truth value.

How is the slippery slope of perspectivistic relativism to be avoided? This can only be done if an epistemic perspective does not present *another* reality, but *another* perspective on the *same* reality, and if reality is understood in such a way that it is disclosed only for particular perspectives that can then engage in a debate about the truth of their respective claims to knowledge. Only if particular perspectives can be understood as being constituted by the subjective certainty concerning the objective truth of a view of reality can they avoid the twofold pitfalls of perspectivistic relativism or a general skepticism, which claims that no certain knowledge of reality can be gained. If the question of truth in the realist sense of the *adaequatio rei et intellectus* is suspended, either because one opts for a relativistic perspectivism or for a general skepticism with regard to all truth claims, then disputes can no longer be debated and approached through the exchange of arguments that are tested against the phenomena of our experience. Every contest of different views becomes a power struggle, which ultimately will be resolved by violence.

These epistemological considerations underline the significance of the question: the same God? If God is the creator of heaven and earth, the ground of all reality, as both Muslims and Christians believe, then the concept of God guarantees the unity of reality. Therefore it would be disastrous if Christians and Muslims would agree that they worship and believe in different gods. This would mean either that Christians and Muslims live in different realities or that there is no unitary ground of all reality. Both possibilities would not allow for a meaningful debate between Muslims and Christians with a chance for mutual understanding (even if it is an understanding of their differences) and for a successful cooperation for common goals, which are recognized by both sides (though, perhaps, on different grounds) as good. However, if it is claimed that Christians and Muslims worship and believe in the same God while they continue to claim either the Qur'ān or Jesus Christ as the ultimate revelation of truth respectively, and both hold that these beliefs are incompatible, this undermines any truth claim that could be associated with God or any meaningful use of the notion of "sameness" and "otherness." The only way out of the dilemma seems to be to insist on the oneness of God and emphasize at the same time that this oneness can only be asserted in different ways from the Christian and the Muslim perspectives so that there can be a real debate on which view of God is true (and the other at least partially wrong). Whereas agreement on the oneness of God is a necessary condition for cooperation in the same reality, consensus in the debate about the sameness of God is not. People can cooperate for the achievement of common goals in the same reality while having very different reasons for it. So, who is to decide? The obvious answer is: only Christians and Muslims can decide from their different respective perspectives of faith.

The Christian Perspective of Faith and the Identity of God

How should Christians then decide from the perspective of Christian faith? This would presuppose to clarify a little more precisely what the perspective of Christian faith is. It is one of the central convictions of Christian faith that the constitution of faith is not a human work, but a work of God the Holy Spirit. Faith is passively constituted *for* humans and not actively constituted *by* humans. However, once faith is passively constituted it is to be actively exercised in the life of faith. Martin Luther has expressed the passive constitution of faith most succinctly in the explanation of the Third Article in the *Small Catechism:*

> I believe that I cannot by my own reason or strength believe in Jesus Christ, my Lord, or come to Him; but the Holy Ghost has called me by the Gospel, enlightened me with His gifts, sanctified and kept me in the true faith; even as He calls, gathers, enlightens, and sanctifies the whole Christian Church on earth, and keeps it with Jesus Christ in the one true faith; in which Christian Church He forgives daily and richly all sins to me and all believers, and at the last day will raise up me and all the dead, and will give to me and to all believers in Christ everlasting life. This is most certainly true.

What is described here as the constitution of faith by the work of the Holy Spirit is commonly summarized by the technical concept of "revelation." This technical concept, which was introduced in late medieval times, expresses the mode of knowledge that is constituted for us by a disclosure experience that constitutes personal certainty of faith. It enables us to become certain about something that we could not actively make known to ourselves. This disclosure experience occurs contingently and affects the whole of our personal being in the world; it grants insight into our existence as personal beings with finite conditioned freedom. Let me state quite bluntly that I believe that the concept of revelation only makes sense if we do not restrict it to a specific religious realm but see it as denoting the general way in which the foundations of our active knowing are constituted for us. In this sense I would argue for a general theory of revelation, and not necessarily for a theory of general revelation.

The passive constitution of Christian faith has a deep significance for the relationship of Christian believers to adherents of other religions who also claim that their religious relationship to God or the ultimate focus of meaning is passively constituted for them and not actively produced by them. It seems to me a decisive characteristic of religions as opposed to ideologies that they claim that their insight is disclosed to them and cannot be actively achieved by human beings. This is the reason why only religions that know the insight of faith is passively constituted can grant one another freedom of religion. The insight of Christian faith into its own constitution, as it is expressed in Luther, is at the same time a decisive self-limitation. On the basis of this insight, Christians know that they can create neither their own faith nor that of others. Creating faith remains exclusively a divine work. However, if this account of the constitution of certainty is true, Christians are committed to the view that this constitution of certainty is not just a special Christian case but applies to all other certainties and to other religious certainties as well. The insight into the constitution of their own faith therefore implies the commitment to tolerate the certainties of others, including that of other religions, since they must suppose that what they claim to be revelation has been disclosed to them in just the same way — although it has not become a revelation for me as a Christian.

The specific content that is disclosed in the revelation which is the foundation of Christian faith is the relationship of our personal being to the ground, goal, and meaning of all created existence. In Luther's explanation of the work of the Holy Spirit it is called the gospel. The gospel is both promise and narrative, the narrative of the person and work of Jesus Christ. What is made certain by the internal testimony of the Holy Spirit is a story that can be told; it is the external word, a message proclaimed in the sign system of human language that has a propositional content and makes definite truth claims. The certainty of faith therefore does not concern some arcane knowledge but a message that can be handed on and understood by the normal means of human communication. Its content is the reconciliation between God and the world, the healing of the broken relationship between God the creator and his estranged human creatures as it is witnessed in Scripture. Certainties cannot be communicated or handed on. They are always person-relative. The truth about which believers are certain can be communicated, albeit not as a vindicated truth claim but as a truth claim. It is this message that is publicly communicable and publicly contestable. This is a matter of Christian witness as well as of interreligious dialogue. Conversation about this message is the medium of discursive rationality for Christians, also in their conversations with other religions.

However, what is witnessed in the gospel of Christ or the message of reconciliation is a message that concerns the relationship of God the creator to his creation; it is a message about the constitution, character, and meaning of the whole of reality. The reality to which the message refers is grounded in the faithfulness of the creator who reestablished created freedom by faith in Jesus Christ. Over against the dislocation of sin in the relationship of humans to God, the gospel is that they are relocated in the relationship to the one who is the creative ground, the reconciling power, and the perfecting goal of everything there is. The reality of creation is therefore the field where the perspective of faith is vindicated and challenged in our dealings with reality. The constant question is: What difference does it make for our understanding of and action in the world that the world is God's creation, that we are destined to exercise our created freedom as God's creatures and as created images of divine freedom through the active self-determination of created freedom? It is this reality of our experience of living in the world as it is understood from the perspective of Christian faith as being shaped by God's creative, reconciling, and perfecting love that provides the testing-ground for the life of faith. The reality of creation, which we share with all other creatures and also with the believers of other religions, is therefore the framework where the truth of faith is put to the test, where it is vindicated, and where it is challenged.

The internal structure of Christian faith, which connects the personal certainty of faith with the public truth claims of the gospel and with the reality to which these truth claims refer, is seen in Christian faith as one structured divine economy that has its unity in the action of the triune God. This whole process from the illumination of the human heart through the gospel of Christ and further to the will of God the creator shows us one unitary, yet differentiated structure of divine action, which connects creation, reconciliation, and sanctification. One of the earliest but also clearest expressions of this connection can be found in Paul: "For it is the God who said, 'Let light shine out of darkness,' who has shone in our hearts to give the light of the knowledge of the glory of God in the face of Jesus Christ" (2 Cor. 4:6). God who is the creator of the primordial light of creation is the one who also illumines our heart so that we can see the glory of God in the face of Christ. There is therefore a comprehensive logic in God's creative action that culminates in the constitution of the knowledge of faith. The author ("the God who said, 'Let light shine out of darkness'"), the content ("the glory of God in the face of Jesus Christ"), and the process ("who has shone in our hearts to give the light of knowledge") of revelation or of the constitution of faith are one in these three distinctive acts.

In the exposition of the Third Article of the Creed in the *Large Catechism,* Luther has summarized this in the following way:

> But here we have everything in richest measure; for here in all three articles He has Himself revealed and opened the deepest abyss of His paternal heart and of His pure unutterable love. For He has created us for this very object, that He might redeem and sanctify us; and in addition to giving and imparting to us everything in heaven and upon earth, He has given to us even His Son and the Holy Ghost, by whom to bring us to Himself. For (as explained above) we could never attain to the knowledge of the grace and favour of the Father except through the Lord Christ, who is a mirror of the paternal heart, outside of whom we see nothing but an angry and terrible Judge. But of Christ we could know nothing either, unless it had been revealed by the Holy Ghost.

What is described here in the language of the threefold divine self-giving or God's threefold gratuitous generosity is, according to Luther, not just the inner logic of divine action, but the depiction of God's Trinitarian being, which can be described by speaking of the personal acts of the persons of the Father, the Son, and the Spirit. The doctrine of the Trinity is based on God's Trinitarian self-presentation, which comprises the author, the content, the process, and the effect of divine revelation. As such, the doctrine of the Trinity is needed to give a complete account of how the constitution of faith enables the act of faith in such a way that the act of faith is enabled and the content of faith is given in God's Trinitarian self-giving.

Let us not avoid the harsh conclusion, which Luther draws from this:

> These articles of the Creed, therefore, divide and separate us Christians from all other people upon earth. For all outside of Christianity, whether heathen, Turks, Jews, or false Christians and hypocrites, although they believe in, and worship, only one true God, yet know not what His mind towards them is, and cannot expect any love or blessing from Him; therefore they abide in eternal wrath and damnation. For they have not the Lord Christ, and, besides, are not illumined and favoured by any gifts of the Holy Ghost.

The Trinitarian faith is here depicted as a radicalization of faith in one God, which also exists outside Christianity. Trinitarian faith is radical monotheism. The insight of faith into God's Trinitarian self-giving says that God is not only the source of the existence of the world, but also the one whose relationship to humans is revealed by Jesus Christ, who as the "mirror of the paternal heart" shows us the "deepest abyss of His [God's] paternal heart" as being "His pure unutterable love."

God is as he presents himself in his threefold self-giving. On this basis Christians know that the one God, who is also believed by "Jews, Turks," even by "false Christians and hypocrites," is in his relationship to his creatures ("what his mind towards them is" — note: not only towards Christians) "pure unutterable love." Not knowing this, because they do not believe in Christ and the Holy Spirit, non-Christians "cannot expect any love or blessing from Him" and "abide in eternal wrath and damnation." This is an astonishing conclusion. Luther says that non-Christians *have* the same God as Christians, because there is only one God and this God is the triune God who revealed himself in his threefold divine self-giving as "pure unutterable love." However, because non-Christians do not believe in Christ and the Spirit they neither *recognize* the true character of God nor do they expect his love or blessing. Since they do not know God in the same way as Christians, they know God in a deficient form. They know God to be one, but are not certain about his relationship to them and about what to expect from him. The conclusion is that, according to Luther, Jews and Muslims, even hypocrites and false Christians *have* the same God, although they do not believe in him or worship him. They do not get beyond the one God because they do not believe in Christ and the Spirit. However, that does not mean that God is for them another God, only that they perceive God without Christ as an "angry judge," and without the Spirit cannot "expect his love or blessing." "Eternal wrath and damnation" are therefore the result of being in the wrong relationship to God, of not knowing God in the way God wants himself to be known.

Revelation, the Hiddenness of God, and the Limits of the Knowledge of Faith

The implications of this view go beyond the way in which Luther himself was able to see the relationship between Christians and Jews, Muslims, other believers, and nonbelievers. How should Christians approach the other religions if they take Luther's view seriously — that they have the same God but that they do not know it? If all God's creatures have the same God, it seems impossible to limit the economy of salvation to the Christian church and leave the rest of the world to other powers. Since the God who is revealed in his threefold divine self-giving is the God of "unutterable love," this must apply to the whole relationship of God to the world, although God can only be known where God makes himself known. How do Christians then relate to the other religions? It seems obvious to me that Christians cannot claim that God is the almighty creator of heaven and earth who is everywhere present to his creation and deny God's presence in the religions. In encountering the religions Christians expect the presence of God in them, the presence of the God who is, as they know God through his self-presentation in Christ and the Spirit, "unutterable love." However, Christians know from their own experience of faith that the presence of God is hidden in the world; it may be obscured by sin and unbelief, an experience they do not only have outside the church but also within the church, since only God knows who the true believers are. In encountering the other religions Christians therefore encounter the hiddenness of God as it is obscured through sin and unbelief, in the church as well as outside the church. It is, however, the hiddenness of the same God that the gospel proclaims. Therefore Christians will expect to experience the same God in new ways also in the religions. The only criterion they have for that is the gospel of Christ, as the way in which Christians believe God revealed himself. The other religions are therefore for Christians neither a Godless zone, nor enemy territory. Christians cannot see the existence of the religions as an operating accident in the history of salvation. What the precise role of the religions is in God's providence has remained hidden until now, but that they must have a role is clear from what Christians believe about the presence of the almighty creator to the whole of creation.

Is there a way of dealing with the tension between God's particular revelation which nevertheless has a universal import and God's general hiddenness, which, however, seems to have a particular meaning although it may elude us now? We can again try to get some inspiration from Luther. In the concluding paragraphs of *On the Bondage of the Will,* Luther employs the popular and good distinction *(vulgata et bona distinctio)* between the light of nature *(lumen naturae),* the light of grace *(lumen gratiae),* and the light of glory *(lumen gloriae).* Luther employs this distinction in order to deal with the dialectics of the knowledge of faith. By the *lumen naturae* we can know that there is a God. However, this light, which Luther frequently equates with reason, cannot help us with the riddles and challenges of our experience in the world. Why should it be just that good people suffer and bad people enjoy a good life? The light of grace tells us that God's justice is not identical with the justice of the world but is a creative and transformative justice. Therefore God's ultimate justice is not yet executed, since this life is only the beginning of the future life. However, there still remains, even in the light of grace, the question why God should condemn those who by their own powers can do nothing but sin. The light of nature and the light of grace cannot fathom why God should give the crown to a godless person without any merits and possibly does not crown or even condemns somebody who is not more godless or even less godless. However, this insoluble difficulty shall be clarified in the *lumen gloriae* where God's justice, which is now incomprehensible, will be made fully manifest.

This distinction clearly suggests limits to the knowledge of faith, which is bound to the light of nature and its transformation in the light of glory. The light of grace only knows that God saves those who are lost because of their estrangement from God, and this transformative justice we can now hope in faith will show to be victorious in the light of glory. How God will disclose himself as the same God, the God who is now known only by the light of grace, remains hidden until God discloses himself fully to everybody. There is a kind of epistemological modesty involved here that does not presume upon the revelation of the light of God's glory.

It seems to be one of the special characteristics of Christian faith that it does not expect the implementation of the truth of faith for all people within history. The goal of history is not that all people will become Christians. The full revelation of God's truth will occur at the end of history. In history we continue to live under pluralistic conditions, and therefore our efforts must be directed at managing the pluralistic situation in the light of faith's apprehension of God's character and of the human destiny.

Tolerance, Dialogue, and Cooperation

We have already seen that the insight into the constitution of their own faith as passively constituted obliges Christians, if this insight is true, to assume that this is also true for other believers. There is therefore a tolerance on the basis of faith, which respects and tolerates the faith of others. Contrary to the demand for tolerance as it has been suggested by the Enlightenment, which is based on the uncertainty of religious faith, this kind of tolerance is based on the certainty of faith. The grounds for this tolerance can therefore be found in the traditions of the different religions. However, on the basis of such a view of the religious roots of tolerance, believers of different religions are not confronted with the demand to be less religious so that they can be more tolerant. Rather, it encourages believers to discover in their own traditions the grounds for being tolerant towards others. In this way, it encourages them to be more religious in order to become more tolerant.

A similar perspectival reasoning can be applied to the theory and practice of interreligious dialogue. Interreligious dialogue has far too long been conducted under the expectation of some sort of consensus, which should be achieved by means of dialogue. If, however, we start from the respective perspectives of faith, we should not engage in conversation with other religions with the (rather oppressive) expectation of reaching some kind of consensus but with the expectation of gaining a better understanding of our differences. This requires that in interreligious dialogues the different religions encounter one another on the basis of their respective self-interpretations (independence condition) and then try to engage in conversation of the basis of their respective understandings of the other (interdependence condition). This provides the opportunity of correcting our understanding of the other through engagement with the other's self-interpretation. There is no given lingua franca for this kind of exchange but only the patient way of understanding the other by the analogical extension of our own perspective of faith. It will involve techniques of translation — translating the others' beliefs into our own framework of understanding and attempting to translate our beliefs into the framework of other religions. It seems to me that we still have to discover the relevance of our respective theologies and the riches of our respective traditions as resources for a dialogue with others.

That seems to me to be especially true for Christian-Muslim relations. What would it mean for Christians to understand the intricacies of Qur'ānic exegesis? What would it mean for Muslims to appreciate that Christian faith is not concerned with a Trinity of God, Jesus, and Mary but with the Father, the Son, and the Spirit? How should Christians (and Muslims) view the fact that the mystic Abu Hasan Ali Ibn Ahmad ad-Dailami (tenth/eleventh century) offered an intricate argument as to why oneness and threeness do not have to be contradictory, since the lover (the mystic) and God (the beloved) are united in the one love? How should Muslims and Christians and Jews, each from their own perspective of faith, interpret these verses from the Qur'ān?

> For each of them we have established a law,
> and a revealed way.

And if God wished,
God would have made you a single nation;
but the intent is to test you
in what God has given you.
So let your goals be everything good.
Your destiny, everyone, is to God,
Who will tell you about
that wherein you differed. (5:48)

The aim of dialogue, it seems to me, will not be a dogmatic consensus. However, much would be gained if it prepared the ground for a cooperation of the religions, especially Jews, Christians, and Muslims, for those aims that from their respective perspectives they recognize as common good. This cooperation will not be based on the recognition of common ground, which for all three monotheistic religions seems very different, but it can be aimed at realizing common goals that will be justified within each tradition by different grounds. Is that the way in which the three monotheistic religions can follow the injunction: "So let your goals be everything good"? It is an exhortation remarkably similar to that of Paul: "test everything: hold fast to what is good; abstain from every form of evil" (1 Thess. 5:21).

We have arrived at a curious conclusion. From the Christian perspective it seems we have to say that Jews, Christians, and Muslims *have* the same God — and this statement would be underlined by Jews and Muslims from the perspective of their respective faiths. However, they each would emphasize that the others do not worship or believe in this God in the same way, because God has been revealed to them, according to their self-understanding, in different ways — which, from each of the perspectives, creates a real difference in worship and faith. However, this difference would not seem to exclude that we live in the *same world,* interpreted from our different perspectives, in which we have to act together for our common good.

Christians, Muslims, and the Name of God: Who Owns It, and How Would We Know?

Denys Turner

The identity of individuals is problem enough in the case of Sir John Cutler's stockings, which, being originally silk, have been continuously darned with wool until none of the silk remains. Are they the *same* socks, even though none of the original matter remains at the end of the process? Of course, if you produce a pair of silk socks from behind your back and then immediately a pair of wool socks, we can be certain that they are not the same pair of socks, because one and the same pair of socks cannot be simultaneously all silk and all wool. But with Sir John's socks it is different; for they have history on their side: intuitively, we are inclined to say that they are the same socks, because what links the end with the beginning is a single, unbroken, spatiotemporal process of change, or, as we might say, a single narrative of space and time coordinates. And if that intuition is correct, then it follows that even with purely material individuals you do not need any actual sameness of matter as a condition of their identity. And that is just as well, given that since Werner Heisenberg's discovery of his "uncertainty principle" the velocities and positions of subatomic particles of matter have themselves been shown to be simultaneously indeterminable. For Newtonian middle-sized material objects, fortunately, all we need is Newtonian spatiotemporal continuities on a middle-sized scale.

In my opinion, sameness of persons is obedient to much the same conditions — at least, speaking as a nondualist. I do not suppose, as a certain kind of Cartesian might, that what makes me at the age of sixty-six to be the same person as a certain Denys Turner was on August 5, 1942, is the sameness of Denys Turner's soul. Or at any rate, since his soul does come into it, it does so because his soul is individuated by his body, which is in turn individuated along the same lines and meeting the same conditions as Sir John Cutler's silk stockings: there is a single unbroken narrative of the spatiotemporal coordinates that make a body to be just *this* body, and so a soul to be the soul of just *this* person. Otherwise, like Thomas Aquinas, I have no idea how a dualist imagines that a soul just on its own terms could be an existent individual. To put it simply, "I am not my soul" — *anima mea non est ego* — as Thomas says in his commentary on 1 Corinthians. For a soul is not a self; my soul is just *how* a self is alive with a certain kind of life, namely human. And I can make no sense of a "how-I-am-alive" that is not a "how-this-body-is-alive," individuated by the body it is the soul of.

I say these things merely so as to set the scene as far as concerns our ordinary, secular concepts of "sameness," and not dogmatically, for I am aware that if the issues about the sameness of individuals are horrendously complex, all the more contested is the kind of solution to them I have just so superficially paraphrased. I raise the issues here as preliminary to a brief reflection upon the following quotation from a Christian authority, who says much the same, I suppose, as most of us here would want to hear said, in support of the proposition that Christians and Muslims believe in, and worship, "one and the same God." Here is what that Christian authority says:

> God, the Creator of all, without whom we cannot do or even think anything that is good, has inspired to your heart this act of kindness. He who enlightens all men coming into this world (John 1.9) has enlightened your mind for this purpose. Almighty God, who desires all men to be saved (1 Timothy 2.4) and none to perish is well pleased to approve in us most of all that besides loving God men love other men, and do not do to others anything they do not want to be done unto themselves (cf. Mt. 7.12). We and you must show in a special way to the other nations an example of this charity, for we believe and confess one God, although in different ways, and praise and worship Him daily as the creator of all ages and the ruler of this world. For as the apostle says: "He is our peace who has made us both one" (Eph. 2.14). Many among the Roman nobility, informed by us of this grace granted to you by God, greatly admire and praise your goodness and virtues. . . . God knows that we love you purely for His honour and that we desire your salvation and glory, both in the present and in the fu-

ture life. And we pray in our hearts and with our lips that God may lead you to the abode of happiness, to the bosom of the holy patriarch Abraham, after long years of life here on earth.[1]

It might surprise you to know that the author of these words was a pope. It will almost certainly surprise you to know that they are the words of a *medieval* pope, Gregory VII, writing in the late eleventh century — in notably more generous terms than his current successor — to the Muslim King Anzir of Mauritania: no soft liberal irenicist this Gregory, nor was he a respecter of persons, for he could require Henry II, the Holy Roman Emperor, to travel to Rome barefooted in the snow in penance for his assertion of imperial claims against the papacy. And what does this pope say? Not only that we, Christians and Muslims, believe and confess the same God, but also that we "praise and worship Him daily as the creator of all ages and the ruler of this world," albeit "in different ways": for Gregory it is with the *lex orandi* as it is with the *lex credendi.* Now I wonder: How can Pope Gregory be so sure of that? What would count as believing, confessing, praising, and worshiping "the same God"? Much to the same point: What would count as Christians and Muslims *not* believing, confessing, praising, and worshiping the same God? Or just generally, how do we *know* that your God and my God are one and the same God? Or, yet again — but this time to ask somewhat more pointedly and less theoretically — are those Malaysian Muslims doctrinally justified, if ecumenically ungenerous, who are giving their Christian compatriots a hard time for taking to themselves the name "Allah," on the grounds that what is in the one case the true God and in the other an idol cannot share the same name?

I do not think these questions are idle. I do not think you can just say: "It doesn't really matter whether we do or do not believe in, or worship, the same God, because what matters is that Christians and Muslims are amicable, do not feel divided over such issues; and if the point is not to be divided over issues of theology, the best way is to avoid entertaining theological issues in the first place. So let the matter rest as to whether we believe in the *same* God, on some agreed criterion of sameness. For in any case, is it not optimistic enough to suppose that we could agree as to the

---

1. Gregory VII, *Letter to Anzir, King of Mauritania,* in Jacques Dupuis, *The Christian Faith in the Doctrinal Documents of the Catholic Church,* 7th ed. (New York: Alba House, 2001), pp. 418-19.

same God when we are faced with the even more dismal prospect that we probably will not agree even as to the appropriate criterion of sameness? So let us not divide over issues that in principle cannot be settled and attend to the more practical matter of how to live in peace, and to the areas of practical action where we can find uncontested common ground, in work for justice and peace in our global village."

This line of response is, I concede, good ecumenical practice in certain circumstances — I mean, often it is good practice to eschew divisive issues of theology *pro tempore* for the sake of practical cooperation over issues on which we can presuppose agreement, if only for the reason that the habits of practical cooperation can create circumstances more favorable to successful doctrinal dialogue than does going for the theological jugular from the outset. But neither Christians nor Muslims can ever more than provisionally detach the theological issues from the practical, justice from the knowledge of God, and soon enough both will want to reengage the one with the other. In any case, though I do know some Christians who seem not to mind theologically if others have got God wrong and worship as God something other than what they themselves worship, it matters to me. And even if I am in a minority among Christians in respect of this theological prescriptiveness, it certainly does matter to most Muslims of my acquaintance. Moreover, I share the Muslim view that others' worship of the wrong God is a sort of offense against mine; indeed, it is just about as fundamental as offenses get, being a form of idolatry. Even if I believe they are wrong to think it so, I can very well see why my belief in the incarnation of the second person of the Trinity in the human nature of Christ matters to a Muslim, for this must seem simultaneously to have introduced multiplicity into the One God and an idolatrous worship of a human person. And I expect most Muslims will understand why their belief that the Word of God is incarnate in the Qur'ān seems to me hard to distinguish from the idolatrous worship of a book, even if they, no doubt, will maintain that I am wrong to do so. In short, I begin from the proposition that in my experience of Muslims I share with most of them, namely, that if it is true that we do, genuinely, disagree about God, then our doing so matters more than anything else at all on which we do happen to agree. So do we disagree about God? More particularly (it is the focus of this paper), do a Muslim's saying "God is one" and a Christian's saying "God is three in one" mean that Christians and Muslims cannot be said to worship the same God — because what the one affirms about God the other denies?

Hick's "Kantian Apophaticism"

There is a way, proposed by John Hick, of construing the differences between Christians and Muslims on the oneness of God, which, without elid-
ing those differences, allows the conclusion nonetheless that they do worship the same God. Now I have the greatest respect for John personally,
and for his views — after all, I was for a few years his successor in the H. G.
Wood Chair of Theology at Birmingham University, and we have been the
very best of friends since. But I think his position is profoundly wrong,
though interestingly it can sound curiously like that of Pope Gregory. Like
Gregory, Hick concedes that we believe in and worship God each in our
"different ways"; but Hick, also like Gregory, believes that it is, to use his
own expression, one and the same "ultimate reality," unknowable in itself,
in which, or in whom, we differently believe and worship.

Of course I cannot here do justice to the subtlety of Hick's argument,
though I would at this point like to interject a note of generalized anxiety
about the conduct of interfaith dialogue in that form in which it takes its
terms from the comparative study of religion. It is obvious, I suppose, that
the category of "religion" is a taxonomical term of principally academic
provenance. I mean, I know of no one at all who actually practices "religion." For sure I don't. I am a practicing Catholic Christian. Speaking for
myself, it bothers me little, one way or the other, if someone within the academic community wants to tell me that, in going to Mass on a Sunday, I
am practicing "religion." It doesn't bother me, because it affects my going
to Mass in no way at all that the academic student of religion wants so to
describe what I am doing there, for there is nothing *internal* to that practice of mass attendance to which that academic's describing it as "religious" makes the least difference. The category of "religion" may be important to the academic, who has other, comparativist, fish to fry. But the
believer needs no such term of art in which to mediate his practice, as the
case may be, of Islam, or Christianity, or Zoroastrianism, or whatever.

What begins to trouble me a bit is when that academic describes the
whole system of belief and practice of Christianity as *a* "religion," if that is
supposed to entail that what makes that belief-system not something else,
say, not a "secular" practice, is some character it has on a comparativist's
common terms with "other" religions. For that would seem to amount to
the claim that what I would find in my faith tradition that makes it "religious" lies either in the lowest common factor (LCF) of belief, symbol, ritual, and practice shared by all "religions," that is, that it consists in a sort of

minimal thread of continuity between them; or else that it lies in something *other than* that which is embodied in the divergent practices of a particular faith, something that, as one might say, they all in some way are said to aspire to, or would ideally converge upon, could they be got to acknowledge the particularity and cultural contingency of their avowed and explicit practice of belief.

Now what seems wrong with the LCF standard of comparison is that the minimum that is common to all "religions" is almost certainly going to be what is least interesting in any of them; and what seems wrong with the "convergent" account of the commonality uniting religions is that it relativizes mine, downsizing to the standing of the provisional what I think of as absolute claims, while offering nothing in epistemic return. For what my and other "religions" are supposed to converge upon will have to be described in terms that are neutral between them all and owned by none. And that, it seems to me, is no basis for any sort of dialogue between them. What that "convergent" understanding of "religion" appears to yield up is a bastard conception of dialogue that, as between any two religious traditions, amounts to a sort of *tertium quid:* a *sui generis* discourse of dialogue standing on its own and additional to the discourses proper to and natural within the faith traditions themselves. It is within this latter conception of the "religious" that it seems right to place Hick's account of it.

As I say, in comments as necessarily brief as these, it is hard not to do an injustice to Hick's way of making the distinction between, on the one hand, the culturally specific and contingent beliefs and ritual practices of Islam and Christianity, and on the other the "ultimate reality" that is the common object of both. But in principle the distinction seems to rely on two different, and in my view incompatible, antecedents, one philosophical and Kantian, the other theological and Eckhartian. The distinction between what in a religious formation is, as it were, "cultural" and contingent and the "ultimate reality" thus diversified by its doctrines and rituals, leaves us with all the epistemological problems of Kant's *Ding an sich.* For, being beyond the reach of all possible description, this "ultimate reality" is an empty category, and its evacuation of all descriptive content offers merely the appearance of providing some common ground — some sameness of God — while at the same time cutting the ground from under any possibility either of affirming or of denying that "sameness." For the absolute unknowableness of "ultimate reality" eliminates all content on which any criteria of sameness and difference can get a grip. After all, if your doctrines of God can no more get a grip on this "ultimate reality" than can mine, the sameness we can be said to share is nothing more than the common possession of a *nescio quid:* we might, in short, be said to share a common ignorance. But I am afraid that if you share with me my complete ignorance of mathematics, it isn't as if there is any mathematics that we can be said to share. All we share is the ignorance, describable as "mathematical" only in the sense that that is what it is ignorance of.

Hick, in more recent writings, however, seems to think that he gains support for his neo-Kantian epistemology in some specifically Christian, and pre-Kantian, "mystical theologies," especially in that radically "apophatic" theology of the fourteenth-century German Dominican, Meister Eckhart. For sure, Eckhart does tempt the Hick-minded comparativist. Indeed, he does distinguish between what he calls *Gott* and the *Gottheit,* between the "God" who is known indirectly as mediated through his/her relation with creation, that is, by analogy derived from the divine effects, and the "Godhead" which is beyond all knowing, even by analogy. Famously, Eckhart even prays to God "that he may set me free from God," where around that second occurrence of "God," naming the God from whom Eckhart wishes to be set free, it has become customary in English translations to insert the device, unavailable to medievals, of scare quotes. And this distinction between "God" and the "Godhead" can seem to be akin to Hick's, as if, on an extension of Eckhart's ground you could say: "God" as known by us, known in this way or that within a particular faith tradition, is a sort of provisional God, whereas the hidden Godhead is beyond all knowledge and description, the same for us all.

Admittedly, Eckhart's distinction between *Gott* and *Gottheit* is misleadingly set out in that famous sermon. But the appropriation of the distinction on Hick's neo-Kantian lines is plausible only on a misinterpretation of it. Eckhart's theological epistemology is much indebted to Islamic and Jewish sources, and especially to Ibn Sina, or "Avicenna," as Eckhart knew of him. Both acknowledge the ultimate unknowability of God, though Eckhart frequently presses this "apophaticism" to rhetorical extremes — especially, it goes without saying, in his intensely rhetorical vernacular sermons. But neither Eckhart nor Ibn Sina ever denies that true affirmative utterances are possible of the one and only God. For neither of them is the apophatic doctrine that we are short of things to say about God, for on the contrary, both maintain that creation is an inexhaustible repertoire of names for God — they agree that there are (at least) ninety-nine of them. The apophatic is no more than the doctrine that true of God as ninety-nine names are, they *all* fall short of him — and let us add that "him" also falls short of God, if only to exactly the same extent as does "her." And I suppose it is all of a piece with this apophaticism to say, as Eckhart does, that if what you mean by "God" is tied up too closely with what we know of God's relationship with creation, then that knowledge "fails" of God. For God would not cease to be God had she or he created nothing at all. For Eckhart, then, the "unknowability" of the Godhead is not the unknowability of something other than "God." The unknowable Godhead is just the other side of the divine knowability, and you cannot get to that *ignorantia* of God unless it is a *docta ignorantia*, an ignorance acquired through the patient amassing of the true names of God, on the other side of which alone the true unknowability of God is reached. That is to say, through knowing alone do you make it into the "cloud of unknowing." That is, you can't get to where the unnameableness of God lies unless you get those true names right. As one might say in Wittgensteinian spirit, you cannot in a sort of fit of apophatic enthusiasm throw the ladder of naming away until you have climbed all ninety-nine rungs on the way to the top of it. Or to deploy a different metaphor, the knowability and the unknowability of God are like shot silk: it is one and the same piece of dyed silk, but the color you see varies, depending on the angle of refraction.

I very much doubt, therefore, that Hick's appeal whether to Kant or to a misinterpreted version of Eckhart solves the problem of the divine "sameness" with any adequacy of fit with the classical traditions of either Christian or Muslim forms of apophaticism. Hick's position, moreover, would seem to leave us with the worst of both worlds from an ecumenical point of view: with an equivocal dividedness unresolved so far as concerns anything we do say about God in our different traditions, and with nothing we can say as to the identity of any "ultimate reality" we could unite on. In short, we need a solution that is more openly dialectical. We need the rough and tumble of argument. We appear to disagree, especially as to the "oneness" of God. But do we? And how could you tell? Is it simply that we do not understand one another and are at cross-purposes, or is the disagreement genuine, such that, agreeing on what would count as the oneness of God, I say God is not in that sense "one" and you say he is? And if there is between us a genuine disagreement, is there agreement between us that that sort of disagreement can be settled on common ground and rules of argument? If we do not occupy the same territory theologically, is there any metatheological common territory on which to settle our disagreements? Or, to put it in other terms, what are the rules for disagreement?

Christians and Muslims: How to Disagree

Undoubtedly Christians and Muslims do disagree about God. But of what kind is their disagreement? Does a Muslim's saying "God is one" and a Christian's saying "God is three in one" mean that Christians and Muslims cannot be said to worship the same God — because what the one affirms about God the other denies? As soon as we ask that question we notice an asymmetry: on the whole, Christian theologians do not believe that the Trinitarian nature of God excludes the Muslim doctrine of the divine oneness, whereas on the whole Muslims believe that it does. We need to know if this is just a misunderstanding on one side or the other, or both, if we are to get anywhere at all with our central question: "Do we believe in the same God?" Let us begin, then, with some clarifications that will help us narrow down the territory of this potential disagreement, for even if we are led to the conclusion that the disagreement is real, there is much in the meantime on which classical Christian and Muslim theologies would appear to agree, at least on a somewhat negative semantic condition, namely that since they agree as to what their respective beliefs rule out, to boot, polytheism, to that extent at least they agree on a meaning for the oneness of God.

What, then, does it mean to say that God is "one"? It means at least two distinguishable things on which Christians and Muslims undoubtedly agree. First, Christians and Muslims believe that there is one and only one God; polytheism is ruled out, and there is no multiplicity *of* gods. Secondly, they are agreed that there is no multiplicity *in* God; God is utterly simple, without composition and without distinction. And in conjunction the two propositions mean that God does not enter into any sort of relations of multiplicity at all. Christians and Muslims agree on ruling out at least that much. When it comes to God there is no counting to do of any kind, and Eckhart is not departing from mainstream Christian theologies in any way when, Trinitarian theologian though he be, he says without qualification: "There is no number in God." How so?

You can look at one side of this "uncountability" in God this way. Suppose, in the conduct of some quite lunatic thought-experiment, you were to imagine counting the total number of things that there are, have ever been, and will be, and you get to the number n. Then I say: "Fine, that's the universe enumerated, but you have left out just one being, the being who made all that vast number of things that is the universe, namely God." And, because you are not an atheist, you agree that this is so. Do you now add God to the list? Is that what I am asking you to do? Does the total number of things that there are now amount to $n + 1$? Emphatically not for Eckhart; and — just in case you were to agree with Pope John XXII, who in 1329 declared Eckhart's theology to be of dubious Christian orthodoxy — emphatically not for the unquestionably orthodox Thomas Aquinas either. For Aquinas is as unambiguous as Eckhart, and says that God's oneness is not such that God is one *more* in any numerable series whatsoever. And this is because both Eckhart and Thomas agree with the pseudo-Denys that "there is no kind of thing that God is." Hence, not being any kind of thing, not being "one of the things that there are," God cannot be counted in any list of the "everything that is." God's oneness is not the oneness of mathematics, as it would be were I, as if equivalently, to say: "I'll have one pie for lunch, not two."

You might object: the oneness of God must be at least minimally mathematical, for it enters into mathematical relations of negation — "ruling out" must come into it again. For however transcendent you may say your understanding of God's oneness is, it must entail the denial of a plurality of gods. You must know at least this much about there being one and only one God: like my one pie for lunch, the oneness of God excludes there being two of them. That, of course, is so, but not for the reason that God's "oneness" excludes plurality in the same way as does the oneness of the numeral "one." What is wrong with saying that there are two, or twenty-two, gods is not that you have added up the number of gods incorrectly. A plurality of gods is ruled out by God's oneness because God's oneness entails that *counting* is ruled out in every way. It is the adding up itself that is mistaken. For if in counting more than one God you get polytheism, in saying that the one and only God is numerably "one" you are neither more nor less mistaken than in saying there are many. Either way you have but idolatry, in a form of which the classical theologies of both Christianity and Islam have long had the measure. Thus far, to the extent that I understand both, Christian and Muslim theologies have no need to quarrel over the oneness of God understood as the denial of polytheism. You need to say two things here on which both traditions are agreed. First, that, as of God, our grip on ordinary senses of oneness is loosened, *perhaps* (as some Christians in the Middle Ages were wont to say) analogically. Second, that if positively God's oneness is beyond our ken, our grip on the divine oneness is not so slack that we cannot know what it excludes.

But does not Christian Trinitarian doctrine reverse all this as regards the divine simplicity, as regards, that is, number *in* God? Granted that an agreed understanding of God's oneness rules polytheism out, does not this Trinitarian understanding of the divine oneness introduce multiplicity and counting into God's inner life by means of its differentiation of persons? Do not Christians say that there are three persons in one God — not two, not four? To make matters worse, do you remember Bernard Lonergan's famous theological equation with which he used to introduce every class at the Gregorian University in Rome: that $5 + 4 + 3 + 2 + 1 = 0$? "In the Trinity," he would say, "there are five 'notions,' plus four 'appropriations,' plus three 'persons,' plus two 'relations,' plus one 'being,' collectively adding up to the zero of the unknowable Godhead." What now about Eckhart's "there is no counting in God," resolutely Trinitarian as his theology is? That Christians do not just happen to say such things, that they are impelled to say them by force of their core doctrine of the Incarnation, can only make matters worse, for that nexus between the doctrines of the Incarnation and of the Trinity, so tight as it is in Christian theology, shows to a Muslim just what is wrong with the doctrine of the Incarnation too. The Muslim responds that you cannot consistently say "God is one" in the sense of being utterly simple, and maintain that Jesus is the incarnation of just one of the three persons. Three persons in one God is an idolatrous oxymoron. In short, Muslim oneness appears to rule out the Christian Trinity.

As I understand it, the Muslim objection to Trinitarian theology — on this point of the logic of theological language — ought not to be thought to rest on the vulgar case, easily dismissed on their own grounds as much as on Christian, that it involves a contradiction of a simple mathematical sort, since it seems to maintain that the personal God who is one and in every way undivided is at the same time divided three ways by a trinity of persons. Of course nothing's being just one in a certain respect can be three in just that same respect. There cannot be more than one Denys Turner, even if, for all I know, there are three people in the telephone directory called "Denys Turner." Now you might think that in speaking of the Trinity of persons in one Godhead nothing more is claimed than to say that there are three instantiations of the divine nature in the same way that three persons called "Denys Turner" are three instantiations of the one human nature. But Christians are not saying that. They are not saying that just as there are three human beings called "Denys Turner," one in New Haven, one in New Canaan, one in Litchfield, three in that they are three persons, one in that all three are human beings; so, in the same way, there are three divine persons, one the Father, another the

Son, and the third the Holy Spirit, albeit one in that each is an individual instance of the divine nature. For that is self-evidently tri-theism and is utterly indefensible, even for Christians, and of course for Muslims. But if Christians are saying anything other than that, then are they not perforce saying that these three persons are one person? And that amounts to a plain contradiction — no mystery there, just muddled nonsense.

Augustine and Thomas Aquinas alike saw that what gets in the way of Trinitarian orthodoxy here is the troublesome word "person." You can see why you need the word theologically; indeed, both Christians and Muslims want to say that God is "personal," for how else than in and through the vocabulary of "person" is the language of knowledge and love to get any purchase on God, which the scriptures of both our traditions not merely warrant but require? But I think it worth pointing out that it is not only for Christian Trinitarians that on our ordinary understanding of it, the word "person" is going to cause trouble. As I say, Augustine and Thomas knew, and do not need instruction from us, that only tri-theistic mayhem would be visited upon their Trinitarian theologies were they to try to work them through on the basis of the standard meanings of "person" available in their own times. More especially Thomas is sensitive to the problems generated by the accepted standard definition of "person," inherited from Boethius, as "an individual substance of a rational nature." It is because he defers to the tradition of translation that renders Nicea's Greek *hypostasis* by the Latin *persona* that he uses the term at all in his Trinitarian theology. And it is because he is made uneasy by the term that he avoids using it whenever he can. The problem is not so much that of the overtones of the word "rational" that could be carried over into a misrepresentation of the divine knowledge (though there is trouble enough in wait there), but because of the implications of the expression "individual substance of" *any* "nature." If there are three Boethian substances in God — individual instantiations of a common nature — then necessarily tritheism follows.

But Muslims should not too eagerly gloat over this Christian theological predicament. If they too want to speak of God as a "person," they had better watch out for the consequences for their own conceptions of the oneness of God. For just as indefensible as Christian tri-theism would be a Muslim account of the oneness of the divine personhood that construed it as the one and only, even as the one and only possible, instantiation of the divine nature. For that, after all, is the condition of the last dodo. The last dodo is of course unique. And being the last one of a species that procreates sexually, it is necessarily unique: there *cannot* be any more. But otherwise than on a merely contingent and *de facto* circumstance such as that of the extinction of all but one dodo, there is no possible sense to the notion that *logically* there can be only one instantiation of a nature. For any nature whatsoever, it is necessarily the case that *logically* it can be replicated. God is not the individuated instance of *any* nature, even of the divine nature: that is what the pseudo-Denys meant when he said that God is not any kind of being. Hence, it is not and cannot be as just one of a kind that God is "one"; but then, neither can it be how the persons of the Trinity are counted as "three." As Eckhart said, "there is no counting in God" — not, as we must now understand him to have meant, as thereby somehow prioritizing the oneness of God over the Trinity, but as a condition equally of nonidolatrous talk of the Trinity and of nonidolatrous talk of the divine oneness. There can be no such counting in God *either* way.

The trouble with talk of persons, whether deployed of the divine Trinity or of the divine oneness, is then, that by force of its natural meaning, in the one case it tends to generate either tri-theistic heresy or plain contradictory nonsense, depending on which way you play it; and in the other it generates an idolatrous conception of God as just a special case of an individuated nature where just one individual exhausts all of that nature's possibilities. And that cannot be what Muslims teach about the divine oneness. And given the requirements of the respective scriptural authorities, in both traditions alike, to speak of the "personal" character of God, we have to ask how much of that natural meaning of "person" can survive its transference upon the divine being. Or, to turn the problem around the other way (it amounts to the same problem), when it comes to the personhood of God, what can be left of our secular notions of *either* oneness *or* threeness?

Given their warnings about the theological trouble caused by a naïve employment of the language of "persons," both Augustine and Thomas resorted to the admittedly more abstract, and certainly humanly less appealing, category of divine relations; not, be it known, to relations *of* or *between* divine persons, but to persons as being *nothing but* relations. That, of course, is hard talk, and the language twists and bends under the pressure of having to say not that the Father generates the Son, but is *the generating of the Son;* not that the Son is *what* is generated by the Father, but is *the being generated by the Father;* and even more awkwardly, not that the Holy Spirit is *what* is "breathed forth," or "spirated," by the Father through the Son, but is *the being spirated by the Father through the Son.* There is nothing here but relatings, no somewhats doing the relating. The language strains. But bent and twisted as the language is, does it break?

Here is an analogy that, like all such analogies, does some good explanatory work so long as it is not thought to do all of it. There is one and only one highway known as the Interstate 95. But it has two directions, one south from Boston to Miami, the other north from Miami to Boston. The direction north is of course really distinct from the direction south, as anyone knows to their cost who has entered the I-95 in the wrong direction a long way from the next exit. And yet both are really identical with the one and only I-95. In this case, we are under no temptation to say that the difference between the direction north and the direction south is just a driver's point of view, because if you are mistakenly traveling to Boston when you want to get to Miami it is the *direction* you need to change, not your point of view. As a Christian theologian might analogously say, "modalism" won't meet the case; the distinction of persons is "real," not notional. But equally, in the case of the I-95, we are under no temptation to say that there are three I-95s, the road north, the road south, and the road that north and south are the two directions of. For the relations of northbound and southbound directions are really identical with one and the same I-95. As we might say, tri-theism is not, on this analogy, entailed.

Of course I admit that this is at best a partial analogy, one designed to allay some initial suspicions concerning the logical consistency of Trinitarian orthodoxy with a resolute defense of the oneness of God. But that the analogy at best limps is shown by the fact that whereas the two directions, north to Boston and south to Miami, are real relations, and are really distinct from one another as relations, the tarmac-covered strip is a real entity, distinct from the directions north and south not as they are distinct from one another, but only as in general any entity is distinct from any relation — in the way, for example, that I am distinct from my being on the right or on the left of this table. And if you were to press my analogy on the doctrine of the Trinity, you might indeed avoid modalism and tri-theism, but you would certainly get out of it some form or other of a heterodox subordinationism — the doctrine that the Father is existentially prior to the Son and the Holy Spirit, just as an entity is existentially prior to the relations that depend on it. And for Christians, Nicean orthodoxy plainly rules that out.

What Nicean orthodoxy requires Christians to say is that Father, Son, and Holy Spirit are all three "relatednesses." And however strange such talk may seem — and it is *extraordinarily* strange — you say it because only on such terms could you say without gross inconsistency both that the three persons are really distinct from one another and really identical with the one, undivided Godhead. But therein lies the point: if, under the pressure of Christian belief, to wit, in the doctrine of the Incarnation, the meanings of "person" and of "threeness" have migrated off the semantic map of our secular vocabularies, so has the Muslim "oneness." For, as we have seen, the oneness of the one personal God of Islam cannot be thought of in terms of the one and only instance of the divine nature either. In either tradition, then, the meanings of "person," "threeness," and "oneness" have all migrated theologically off the same semantic map, and to the same extent. To which conclusion I would add only this rider: that it is much easier for a Muslim than it is for a Christian to forget this, as if the "oneness" of God were easier to get into your head than the Trinity. It isn't.

Getting the "Apophatic" Right

At this point it is tempting on both sides to appeal to the "apophatic" distance between God and any creatures or any creaturely analogy. This was Augustine's move — it surprises some, though it shouldn't — that in Book 15 of his *De trinitate,* where, having for fourteen books played out his analogy between the soul's highest powers and the persons of the Trinity for all its worth, he concludes that of course it doesn't work; or, as in his more compendious way, Lonergan did, who after piling up on top of one another all fifteen of the Trinitarian enumerations concluded that they added up to a zero, cognitively speaking. Well, as we will see, we do have to make some such appeal. God *is* a mystery, and I think it fair to say that the best theologies in either faith tradition are designed not to eliminate, but on the contrary, to safeguard, the mystery which God is. But, as we saw with Hick, it is essential to get the mystery of God in the right place. And there are two ways of getting it in the wrong place. You have certainly misplaced it if what you say in your theology amounts to forms of contradiction detectable by the means of ordinary logic. Plain contradictions are not apophatic: they are simply nonsense. Contradictions do not point to mysteries beyond our understanding. They simply fail to point.

On the other hand, if the appeal to the apophatic is meretricious in support of plain nonsense, neither can we allow the Hickian move, which simply shifts the problem over to the other horn of the dilemma. There is no way out of the apparent conflict between Islam and Christianity on the question of the oneness and threeness of God simply by evacuating both of all such content as *could* entail a contradiction. That would be no more justifiable an appeal to the "apophatic" than would Hick's; indeed it would be wrong for exactly the same reason. That is to say, just as Hick's "ultimate reality" conflicts with nobody's theology because *a fortiori* there can be no knowable descriptions true of it to conflict with anything, so concepts of the divine oneness and of Trinitarian threeness — which have no consequences for counting in God — gain an ecumenical reduction in conflict by the device of nothing's being asserted on either side. But both Christian and Muslim doctrines of God do, as we have seen, have some exclusionary consequences for counting: for Christians there are three persons in one God, not two or four; and for both Christians and Muslims, there is one God and not two or twenty-two. For both alike, the simplicity of God is preserved; for both alike, everything true of God *is* God.

So have we made any progress at all? Certainly some, but not very much. But then I am not sure how much progress we should expect to have made. At its most pessimistic you might say that all I have achieved so far is a sort of logical throat-clearing, nothing yet having been offered positively, but only what will *not* do by way of an answer to the question, "Do Christians and Muslims believe in the same God?" On the Christian side we have apophatically to say that our way of counting persons in God is a pretty offbeat sort of counting, since it is not really persons, because not really individuals in any countable sense, that we are talking about; and yet, those Christians cannot so apophatically evacuate the divine threeness as to disable their entitlement to say: "three, not two, not four." And the case matches up on the Muslim side. Muslims must place an apophatic restriction on their "oneness" of God, for they know that it cannot be as you might count the number of Gods so that you know there is only one, even if they also know better than to be so apophatically extreme about the divine oneness as to disable their right to reject polytheism. But that being so, it is on their own account of the divine oneness that Muslims should beware of concluding that Christians merely contradict themselves when they say that there are three persons in one God, or that they thereby compromise the divine oneness. Muslims might have other reasons to say that Christians are wrong about God, perhaps even that they are idolatrously wrong. But what Christians claim about the Trinity does not at least contradict what Muslims say about the divine oneness.

But are they the *same* God? What little my argument at best demonstrates is that Christians and Muslims meet a *necessary* condition for the sameness of the God they confess and worship, namely that both rule out the same contraries (all plurality *of* gods and all plurality *in* God) and that neither need rule out the other in so doing. But I have made no attempt to meet those sufficient conditions for sameness that would be required to establish that Christians and Muslims do worship the same God. That is simply because I do not know what those conditions are — I don't know how to describe them, though I do believe that, whatever they are, they can and will be met in what Christians call the "beatific vision" and both call "paradise." This plea of ignorance is not a merely English conceit of academic modesty. I mean, I really don't know what those conditions are. But then I am not pretending to think you don't know what they are either. Really you don't. And this is because, as I have said, all our secular criteria for identity are disabled regarding God, whether these are appropriate for silk or wool stockings or for the identity of persons. For if we cannot say that God is in any ordinary, secular sense an *individual,* then it follows that we cannot employ our standard secular criteria to establish individual sameness. Likewise, if we cannot say that the three persons of the Trinity are in any ordinary sense three "somewhats," then it does not seem clear on what grounds you could say that they are not each identical with the one undivided God. That being said, the question of whether it is true that there are three persons in one God is rationally undecidable, a matter of faith, of what is or is not revealed. Of course, then, Christians do not and cannot claim to know *how* there could be three persons in one God. But then, the oneness of God is no less beyond our understanding too. And it is just for that reason that it seems impossible to come up with any knock-down way of establishing the identity of the Christian and Muslim Gods, as if, like the two pairs of socks, I could produce a pair from behind my back, and then do it again, and ask you to compare them for identity.

But if, short of the beatific vision in which we Christians and Muslims can hope to share, I am skeptical of any conclusive demonstration of sameness, there is something else I can do — and I hereby do it. I can offer a challenge, to both Christians and Muslims, to come up with a way of showing that when in Malaysia both call upon "Allah" they are *not* calling on the same God. That is, I challenge them to provide such demonstration of their dismissals of the other's claims on that name as, each on their *own* terms, does not presuppose or entail a reductively idolatrous and fundamentalist betrayal of their own best traditions. For my part, I will offer no prize for the best entry. That would be unfairly to rig the competition. For if I am right it cannot be done at all.

And that's because, in concluding on what will seem an excessively downbeat note, I have not told the whole story.[2] Not by a long chalk. Not, however, because I could have told it but didn't, but because it cannot be told at all and because there is only an idolatrous and reductive betrayal in the attempt to tell it. Indeed, all along in this paper that has been my point, namely, that short of the beatific vision the whole story does not lie within our pre-mortem power to tell. And also my point has been to argue for that impossibility, or maybe just to exhibit it, because it is essential to know that we cannot tell the whole story, and because it is essential not only that we do our theologies, but also that we live our lives, under the constraint of that impossibility. To possess the whole story is possible only within the beatific vision; indeed being able to tell it *is* paradise. So if it is so important to know that we cannot for the nonce tell it, it is just as important to know that it is there to be told and that one day we will find ourselves partaking in the unimaginable joy of its telling.

As Dante knew. Folco, in Dante's *Paradiso,* tells us that there within the vision of God, where at last all see and all is seen and, being seen, all is thereby redeemed, "we do not remember our fault, here we simply smile"[3] at the "art that makes beautiful the great result."[4] Within that "great result," Folco tells us, he can afford to forget that which on earth he had need to be weighed down by, the memory of his sins. And so in paradise he can afford to smile. And we, like Folco, will be able simply to smile at our sins, because then, without either excusing or trivializing their depravity, they can no longer weigh us down, can place no burden of guilt upon memory. And as it will be with our sins so will it be for our presently unresolved theological divisions. Then together we will be able to do what we cannot do now. For now we must remember them; there is no honesty in a premature attempt to forget them. Only then will we be able to smile at those divisions — with smiles far removed from the raucous laughter of those who ridicule them, as if it had been only for foolishness that those divisions had mattered to us. For they *did* matter. We could not have abandoned them without loss of such truth as was then possible for us. For now we must live with those divisions, sure only of a common hope that they will be over-

---

2. An earlier version of this paper concluded at the end of the last paragraph. I wrote this revised conclusion after a conversation with Elena Lloyd-Sidle, a Muslim student at the Yale Divinity School. She made me think of Dante's Folco. I am deeply grateful to Elena for that conversation.

3. *Paradiso,* 9, 103-4.

4. *Paradiso,* 9, 106-7.

come, that memory redeemed will be able to tell a healing narrative that we cannot now tell. But in paradise we will look one another in the eye and simply smile at the glint that we see there. Then we will smile with the joy of memory healed, with the joy that we each see in the eyes of the other at our divisions at last resolved. Then, indeed, but for now, not yet.

The Same God?

Amy Plantinga Pauw

The Difficulty of Supplying Grounds

"If someone asked us 'but is that true?' we might say 'yes' to him; and if he demanded grounds we might say 'I can't give you any grounds, but if you learn more you too will think the same.'"[1] It is tempting to give a Wittgensteinian answer to the question, "Is it true that Jews, Christians, and Muslims worship the same God?" In his book *On Certainty*, Wittgenstein warns us against assuming that we can use a one-size-fits-all set of rational criteria for adjudicating what it is we know and believe. What counts as good grounds for some kinds of belief does not count as good grounds for others. That there *are* good grounds for some of our beliefs does not mean that we should expect to find good grounds for all of them.

"A main cause of philosophical disease," Wittgenstein asserts, is "a one-sided diet" — nourishing our thinking with only one sort of example.[2] The question "Is this the same . . . ?" comes up a lot in human life. Are

---

1. Ludwig Wittgenstein, *Über Gewissheit*, ET: *On Certainty*, ed. G. E. M. Anscombe and G. H. von Wright; trans. Denis Paul and G. E. M. Anscombe (Oxford: Basil Blackwell, 1969), Entry 206, p. 28e. Further references to *On Certainty* will be made parenthetically within the text, using the abbreviation OC, followed by the entry number. All references will be to the English translation.

2. Ludwig Wittgenstein, *Philosophische Untersuchungen*, ET: *Philosophical Investigations*, ed. G. E. M. Anscombe and R. Rhees, trans. G. E. M. Anscombe (New York: Macmillan, 1953), Entry 593, p. 155e.

those two wearing the same dress? Are we thinking about the same house? Is he the same Daniel I knew in elementary school? The grounds on which I might argue sameness in each case differ significantly. Would it not be reasonable to assume that grounds for affirming sameness in the case of God would be radically different still, if it were even possible to find any?[3] Might it not be appropriate to say with Wittgenstein that affirming that Jews, Christians, and Muslims worship the same God is a matter of learning more, rather than of supplying grounds?

For some of our most firmly held beliefs, Wittgenstein notes, we do not have anything like adequate grounds: "I cannot say that I have good grounds for the opinion that cats do not grow on trees or that I had a father and a mother" (OC, 262). In many cases our beliefs are stronger than any grounds we can adduce to support them. I can produce historical, devotional, ethical, and philosophical grounds for believing that Jews, Christians, and Muslims worship the same God, but it is not clear that I am more certain of these grounds than I am of the original belief. "At the foundation of well-founded belief," declares Wittgenstein, "lies belief that is not founded" (OC, 253).

Jointly assenting to the claim that Jews, Christians, and Muslims worship the same God does not oblige the three traditions to find grounds on which they can all agree. Jews and Muslims will each have their own grounds for assenting to the claim that the three faith traditions worship the same God. Christians can, however, learn from the grounds they put forward, and may find interesting convergences with distinctively Christian grounds. In the next section I will be pursuing this theological task as a Christian.

The Christian Argument from Creation

The grounds I offer for the claim that Jews, Christians, and Muslims worship the same God are an implication of my belief in God as creator of all.

---

3. Rowan Williams begins an article on identity and change within the Christian tradition in the context of feminist theological challenges with similar everyday examples, and concludes, "If we think of circumstances where we ordinarily discuss identity and continuity, it is clear that some or most of the appeals we might make in such a context do not apply if we are talking about God." "'Is It the Same God?' Reflections on Continuity and Identity in Religious Language," in *The Possibilities of Sense,* ed. John H. Whittaker (Basingstoke, UK; New York: Palgrave, 2002), pp. 204-18, here p. 204.

In the words of the Presbyterian *Brief Statement of Faith* (1993), I believe in "One God, maker of heaven and earth, whom alone we worship and serve." This Christian affirmation is of course indebted to the theological traditions of Judaism, and is also shared with Muslims. It functions as the theological precondition for the distinctive stories each tradition tells of God's relation to humanity: the Jewish, Christian, and Muslim narratives of God's revelation to and blessing of humanity are each built on the conviction that the one God is the source and ongoing sustainer of all life. That this affirmation, at least in its thin, abstract form, is something the three traditions can agree on makes it reasonable for Christians to be favorably disposed at the outset to the claim that Jews and Muslims worship the same God. This would not be true, for example, in the case of traditions that are polytheistic or assert that the world was made by a kind of demiurge. However, rather than seeking theological grounds in a lowest-common-denominator approach, I will proceed by plumbing distinctively Christian understandings of God as creator of all.

Christians confess belief in "*One* God, maker of heaven and earth." The oneness of God the creator is less a numerical observation than a confession of God's radical otherness. God is the sovereign creator of all, not, in the scathing words of H. R. Niebuhr, "someone we try to keep alive by religious devotions, to use for solving our personal problems, for assuring us that we are beloved."[4] God's reality is not dependent on human religious constructions. Asking whether Jews, Christians, and Muslims address the *same* God in worship is thus a bit of a trick question. God, as understood by Christians, is not a member of a well-populated set, or a certain "kind" of object. It is reasonable to argue about whether two people are praising the same movie. In the case of God, however, I have every reason to believe that those who claim to be monotheists are worshiping the same God I am, even if their theologies diverge. The alternative is not that they are worshiping a "different" creator of heaven and earth, but that they are idolaters, failing to worship the one God at all, worshiping instead some part of creaturely reality. Christians have sometimes been quick to label other monotheists idolaters — John Calvin sometimes made this reckless charge against fellow Christians who were Catholics, for example — but the grammar of Christian belief (not to mention Christian charity) militates against this. It is more "grammatical" (if not more charitable) for

---

4. H. R. Niebuhr, "The Anachronism of Jonathan Edwards," in *Theology, History, and Culture,* ed. William Stacy Johnson (New Haven: Yale University Press, 1996), p. 132.

Jews, Christians, and Muslims to label each other heretics — that is, those who worship the one true God, but in fundamentally flawed ways. However, I will argue that Christian understandings of God as creator cultivate instead the virtues of humility, generosity, and hopefulness in our interreligious dealings.

One of the chief obstacles to affirming that Jews, Christians, and Muslims worship the same God is the presence of irreducible theological differences among them. Honesty and respect towards our religious neighbors will not permit ignoring or denying these differences. However, the radical distinction between the one Creator and all creation posited by Jews, Christians, and Muslims paradoxically supports arguments that they worship the same God by indicating the impossibility of capturing God's reality in our theological conceptualities.[5] In Jewish, Christian, and Muslim traditions, as David Burrell likes to put it, God is not just "the biggest thing around," as measured by creaturely categories and concepts. Because all of our human resources are by definition inadequate when it comes to confessing faith in God, believers have to stretch and tear human language and concepts in an attempt to make them serviceable. God's reality always immeasurably exceeds our words and ideas. Christians can hear in Jewish and Muslim theologies the same stammering and groping for truth that we experience in our own theological tradition. It is not the case that each tradition claims a perfectly articulated, unclouded vision of God, so that a side-by-side comparison would be all that is needed to determine their compatibility. For Jews, Christians, and Muslims, God is never an object for human beings to scrutinize but rather an active subject who encounters us in mysterious and surprising ways. As a Christian, I confess with the church that all believers still see God "through a glass darkly" (1 Cor. 13:12); as a result, faulty theological assumptions and even ingrained error may coexist with genuine faith in the one, true God. Because God is not just "the biggest thing around," large and irreducible differences in theological understanding do not automatically nullify the affirmation that the three traditions worship the same God.

It is worth noting that large and seemingly insurmountable differences in understandings of God occur not only *across* different religious

5. David Burrell finds "the distinction" most clearly articulated in Christian theology, as a result of distinctive Christological pressures; but he also finds it in Jewish and Muslim reflection. See David B. Burrell, "The Christian Distinction Celebrated and Expanded," in *The Truthful and the Good: Essays in Honor of Robert Sokolowski*, ed. John J. Drummond and James G. Hart (Dordrecht: Kluwer, 1996), pp. 191-206.

traditions. They also come up *within* religious traditions. When I read portrayals of God by my fellow Christians Tim LaHaye and Jerry Jenkins in their *Left Behind* series, for example, I have difficulty recognizing the God I worship. In fact, I sometimes find it easier to identify theologically with portrayals of God by some members of other religious traditions, for example those by Rabbi Jonathan Sacks. Though we are members of the same religious tradition, Tim LaHaye and I have gone down markedly different exegetical and theological paths, and as a result I often find his portrayals of God puzzling or offensive. But this difficulty does not make me inclined to doubt that Tim LaHaye and I worship the same God, even when I would seem to have reasons to doubt this. My confidence that we after all believe in the same God is grounded less in a side-by-side comparison of our theologies than in the larger constellation of my Christian convictions. I believe that we have both been brought by baptism into Christ's body, a body with many different members. I believe that we are responding to the same summons to discipleship, and that obedience to that summons requires me to approach my fellow Christians with a generous spirit, confident that the Spirit of Christ is at work in them and that God has gifts to give me through them. In this area, as in so many others, I walk by faith and not by sight, trusting that in Christ all Christians have in fact been made one, even when there is much that seems to divide us. While these explicitly Christian rationales do not all translate in the case of theological differences among Jews, Christians, and Muslims, I can still appeal to creaturely finitude and divine otherness to argue that the large theological differences among us are not *prima facie* grounds for doubting that we worship the same God.

Within a Christian theological framework, the affirmation that the one God is maker of heaven and earth refers to a divine self-determination arising out of the fullness and perfection of the eternal triune life. The triune God wills that there should be a finite, creaturely counterpart to the unqualified joy and eternal self-giving that is God's reality *ad intra*. Christian theology holds together God's creative and redemptive work. Christians have seen that the grace poured out in Jesus Christ is not a narrow or stingy grace: it is given freely and without condition. The power, generosity, and freedom displayed in this redemptive love give them a window on God's work as creator. God's creative work, too, is an unconditioned gift. This theological framework portrays the God who gives human creatures life and draws them into relationship as free, faithful, and generous. As we will see, each of these qualities suggests that God is not known and loved by Christians alone, and predisposes Christians to cultivate humility, hopefulness, and generosity toward the theological claims of Jews and Muslims.

God's freedom is predicated on God's otherness and self-sufficiency as creator. The triune God stands in a relation of asymmetrical dependence to all that is. All creation depends on God for its very existence, but God does not depend on it; even the creator-creature distinction itself is the result of God's free agency. This means that God does not create or interact with humanity out of some need or lack on God's part, or because God is propelled by some external force. Christians stand on common ground with Jews, Muslims, and the rest of humanity in our utter dependence on God: God's constant energy and action sustain everything that exists. Divine freedom reminds Christians that God does not need us to be God, and thus that we can claim no inherent divine obligation towards us, much less any monopoly on God's favor. "'Are you not like the Ethiopians to me, O people of Israel?' says the Lord. 'Did I not bring Israel up from the land of Egypt, and the Philistines from Caphtor and the Arameans from Kir?'" (Amos 9:7). Divine freedom prompts humility in Christian self-understanding vis-à-vis other religious traditions. We confess God as the source of all truth, including all true knowledge about God. When Jews and Muslims claim to know and love the One God, maker of heaven and earth, a Christian acknowledgment of God's freedom leads us to trust their claims.

God's faithfulness as creator clarifies that divine freedom is not to be construed as arbitrariness or unpredictability. God is "at one," not torn by conflicting impulses. God is self-consistent in all God's dealings with humanity, faithful even when human creatures are rebellious and ungrateful, and even when they are resentful of God's faithfulness towards others. "If we are faithless, he remains faithful — for he cannot deny himself" (2 Tim. 2:13). God's faithfulness as creator of all that exists must serve as the baseline of Christian understandings of God's particular faithfulness towards us. We have been perennially tempted to construe divine faithfulness towards us as a reward for the faithfulness of the Christian community, a special divine favor towards those who alone know and worship God aright. This construal has necessitated a supersessionist view of our relation to God's people Israel, even though the logic of this supersessionism contradicts the very divine faithfulness it claims: If God has broken covenant promises to Israel, how can God's commitment and forgiveness be trusted in our own case? God's faithfulness to us in Christ should be seen instead as a strategy within the overall economy of divine blessing, not an exclusive divine acknowledgment of our right belief. God's bent is toward the well-being of the entire creation, and the faithfulness of God in bestowing particular gifts to Israel and through Jesus Christ belongs within this larger frame of reference. Knowing God's particular faithfulness to us against the backdrop of God's faithfulness as creator, we are predisposed to accept and even rejoice in Jewish and Muslim praise for God's faithful and providential dealings with them. We trust God's faithfulness to our fellow children of Abraham, even when our comprehension of this "providential diversity of religions" falls short.[6] We hope for what we do not see.

God's creative activity is characterized by generosity: the abundance and diversity of the world reflect the wideness of God's purposes for creation's flourishing. God's self-consistency and faithfulness are not in service to the unity and exclusive welfare of a particular people or nation.[7] The praise and devotion of Jews and Muslims should be taken as evidence of God's generosity to them, and should stir in Christians new gratitude to God. Christian trinitarianism encourages a distinctive understanding of divine generosity as embodying a deep responsiveness and receptivity. As Rowan Williams says, Christian faith has a "picture of the divine life involving receiving as well as giving, depending as well as controlling." The incarnation of God in Jesus Christ shows us that "what we understand by 'God' can't just be power and initiative; it also includes receiving and reflecting back in love and gratitude."[8] This intratrinitarian dimension of God's generosity likewise shapes the contours of our own generosity in estimations of God's work and presence within other communities of faith. Unlike missional paradigms in which Christians are always the ones sent, always the ones called to give witness to the truth, Christian understandings of generosity within God's own life call us to expectations of receiving and depending on others. Joyful receptivity and responsiveness towards the faith of our closest religious relatives is one way we acknowledge and mirror divine generosity.

It will be clear by now that the "grounds" I have provided for assert-

6. J. A. DiNoia, *The Diversity of Religions: A Christian Perspective* (Washington, DC: Catholic University of America Press, 1992).

7. This is not to argue that the three monotheistic faiths have consistently resisted the temptation to make this argument. See Regina M. Schwartz, *The Curse of Cain: The Violent Legacy of Monotheism* (Chicago: University of Chicago Press, 1997).

8. Rowan Williams, *Tokens of Trust: An Introduction to Christian Belief* (Louisville: Westminster John Knox, 2007), pp. 66, 68.

ing that Jews, Christians, and Muslims worship the same God fall well short of a generally convincing argument. I have addressed my argument to fellow Christians, insisting that our own theological convictions provide grounds for trusting the claims of Jews and Muslims to worship the "One God, maker of heaven and earth." My argument thus diverges from what is commonly called a *pluralist* approach. Pluralists often regard it as a kind of moral imperative for enlightened Christians to see "the great religious traditions as different ways of conceiving and experiencing the one ultimate divine reality."[9] They usually proceed to ground this claim by attempting to stake out a theologically neutral common ground that is more basic than the elaborations of any particular theological tradition, and then encouraging particular traditions to relinquish claims that stand in the way of their constructed consensus. I have instead tried to supply distinctively Christian grounds for resisting the domestication of the God we worship, and for trusting in a divine generosity that exceeds our own theological understanding. Rather than asking Christians to minimize the elements in their doctrine of God that set them apart from Jews and Muslims (such as the notion of receptivity and dependence within the divine life, for example), I ask them to plumb these distinctive riches to provide grounds for approaching Jewish and Muslim theological claims and religious practice with humility, generosity, and hopefulness. The freedom, faithfulness, and generosity of the God I know in Jesus Christ through the power of the Holy Spirit lead me to acknowledge the authenticity of other claims to know and love God. Because of the particularities of my Christian faith, not in spite of them, I am justified in taking Jews and Muslims at their word when they profess to worship the "One God, maker of heaven and earth." In short, I have tried to sketch grounds for a sympathetic, generous construal of their religious practice that does not require downplaying theological differences.

If these grounds seem underwhelming, it should be noted that the grounds I offer for my conviction that Jews, Christians, and Muslims worship the same God should not be confused with the *source* of my conviction. The grounds for believing that these three communities worship the same God are a bit like the grounds I might offer for being a Christian. I can set some out, and in certain contexts, it might be important to offer reasons why Christian faith is not wholly implausible or irrational. But those grounds are not the source of my Christian faith. For this, I would

---

9. John Hick, *Problems of Religious Pluralism* (New York: St. Martin's, 1985), p. 102.

point to the work of the Holy Spirit through the various means made available in the practices of the Christian community. Reminiscing about her journey to Jewish faith, Allegra Goodman writes,

> And yet, inexorably, some of my own religion rubbed off on me. Might that be the way belief works for some people? Not a sudden epiphany, but a long, slow accumulation of Sabbaths. No road-to-Damascus conversion but a kind of coin rubbing, in which ritual and repetition begin to reveal the credo underneath.[10]

I suspect that the cause of my belief that Jews, Christians, and Muslims worship the same God is likewise a "slow accumulation of Sabbaths." As in the case of my own coming to Christian faith, I attribute this process to the work of the Holy Spirit. Prayer and theological reflection, and above all common projects with and sympathetic listening to Jews and Muslims, have gradually "revealed the credo underneath." As a result of these practices and experiences, I find myself with the conviction that we worship the same God. But I would not point to these practices and experiences as grounds for that conviction.

Offering grounds is a second-order exercise. Most of the time the claim that Jews, Christians, and Muslims worship the same God seems to function, not as a conclusion reached on the basis of clearly argued grounds, but rather, as the "scaffolding of our thoughts" (OC, 211). For example, we can see the claim functioning in this way in the recent interfaith statements *Dabru Emet, A Common Word between Us and You,* and *A Common Word for the Common Good,* produced by Jews, Muslims, and Christians, respectively. While it is a worthwhile exercise to articulate grounds for the claim that Jews, Christians, and Muslims worship the same God, this exercise is not a prerequisite for using the claim as scaffolding for interfaith explorations.

Thin and Thick Theology

In the face of divine mystery that immeasurably exceeds human powers of comprehension, Christian theologians from St. Paul forward have tended to shift into doxology when their theological arguments run aground (cf.

10. Allegra Goodman, "Counting Pages," *The New Yorker,* June 9 and 16, 2008, p. 90.

Rom. 11:33-36). Recognizing the chronic inadequacy of their theological articulations of God's reality, Jewish, Christian, and Muslim believers have always insisted that God is known most deeply in worship. However, the practice of worship itself presents a deep paradox in theological reflections on whether Jews, Christians, and Muslims worship the same God, for in worship, Jews, Christians, and Muslims feel at the same time the deepest commonalities and the deepest differences.

When Jews, Christians, and Muslims witness each other at worship, they instinctively recognize their deep connections. Worship provides the keenest and most visible common acknowledgment of their existence as creatures oriented in dependence and gratitude towards God their creator. They feel the common impact that God's active presence has on them, despite their theological differences. Prayer to God that confesses sin, expresses devotion, and offers heartfelt praise is one of the deepest impulses of all three faiths. In the Muslim discipline of fasting and Jewish songs of praise, Christians find deep resonances with our own expressions of costly devotion and joyful adoration of God. And yet at the same time, worship is where the particularities of each faith are most clearly brought to the fore. Worship practices distill the distinctive narratives of God's presence with each community. That is why interfaith worship that reaches for a lowest common denominator is so bland and unsatisfying. It fails to nourish and be fed by the deepest springs of religious faith and conviction.

When I as a Christian witness the worship of devout Jews on Yom Kippur or devout Muslims during Ramadan, I feel what Krister Stendahl called "holy envy." I admire the kind of devotion to God that is expressed and made possible within the specific contours of their faith traditions and practices. But I admire it while recognizing that those particular spiritual excellencies are beyond my grasp. They are not available to me any more than the particular forms of devotion to God made possible by cloistered Christian communities are possible for me to obtain as a married person with children. Worship both transcends and reinforces the theological differences among Jews, Christians, and Muslims.

In worship, the three faith communities declare their belief in "One God, maker of heaven and earth." However, this belief is the theological equivalent of what Michael Walzer has referred to as "thin" moral agreement, or a "moral minimum." In his book *Thick and Thin: Moral Argument at Home and Abroad,* he introduces "two different but interrelated kinds of moral argument — a way of talking among ourselves, here at home, about the thickness of our own history and culture . . . and a way of talking to people abroad, across different cultures, about the thinner life we have in common."[11] Similarly, intramural theological agreement among Christians will be thick: "richly referential, culturally resonant, locked into a locally established symbolic system or network of meanings."[12] Theological agreement across religious traditions is by contrast thinner, focused on convergence points "that are seen to be similar even though they are expressed in different idioms and reflect different histories and different versions of the world."[13] In worship the thin convergence around God as creator is embedded within the thick theological traditions of each community of faith.

In this essay I have attempted to support thin theological agreement across traditions by appeal to thicker theological grounds that emerge from within a particular tradition. Thin theology follows and abstracts from thick theology. Walzer insists that it is a mistake to think that men and women everywhere begin with some common idea or principle or set of ideas and principles, which they then work up in many different ways. They start thin, as it were, and thicken with age, as if in accordance with our deepest intuition about what it means to develop or mature.[14]

Rather, he insists, "morality is thick from the beginning," becoming thin for special occasions of solidarity. "We march for a while together, and then we return to our own parades." Similarly, agreement among Jews, Christians, and Muslims that they worship the God who is creator of heaven and earth is a theological minimum. It provides a basis for them to come together, but "by its very thinness, it justifies [them] in returning to the thickness that is [their] own."[15] Even Christian accounts of this theological minimum will always reflect the distinctiveness of our thick theology. There is no theological Esperanto. Or rather, just as Esperanto is much closer to European languages than to any others, so any attempt to construct a theological version of Esperanto will inevitably reflect particular thick theological traditions.[16] A theological version of Walzer's approach is both more respectful of genuine theological difference and more reflective of their particular historical trajectories.

11. Michael Walzer, *Thick and Thin: Moral Argument at Home and Abroad* (South Bend, IN: University of Notre Dame Press, 1994), p. xi.

12. Walzer, *Thick and Thin*, p. xi.

13. Walzer, *Thick and Thin*, p. 17.

14. Walzer, *Thick and Thin*, p. 4.

15. Walzer, *Thick and Thin*, p. 11.

16. Walzer, *Thick and Thin*, p. 9.

Walzer insists that the minimal morality that different peoples share is not substantively insignificant or emotionally shallow — "this is morality close to the bone. . . . In moral discourse, thinness and intensity go together."[17] Likewise, agreement that Jews, Christians, and Muslims worship the "One God, maker of heaven and earth" is significant and powerful. But it is dependent on and arises from the full-fledged theologies of the three faith communities.

In keeping with Walzer's recognition of the importance of "thick" discourses, the Scriptural Reasoning movement has pioneered a promising avenue for deep interfaith sharing. Jews, Christians, and Muslims meet to read and discuss specific texts from their respective scriptures, meditatively reading the text together and then exploring its various meanings. As David Ford notes, through intense focus on each other's scriptures, participants learn "to recognize the strength of our bonds in the family of Abraham and the call to live patiently with our deep differences; and throughout to conduct our reading according to an ethics, and even politics, of justice, love and forgiveness."[18] Here humility, hopefulness, and generosity about each other's deepest faith convictions can thrive.

In these kinds of interfaith discussions, the thin common conviction that Jews, Christians, and Muslims worship the same God is gradually thickened by a deeper awareness of their indebtedness to one another. Understandings of God within any religious tradition can never claim to be fully "homegrown." They are always, to a degree that is impossible to measure precisely, imported from or at least genetically modified by the traditions of other religious communities. That is particularly true for the Christian tradition, which developed *in media res,* after the foundational covenants of Judaism, but before the claims of Mohammed's privileged prophetic status for Islam. From the beginning to end, Christian views of God have been indebted to those of their fellow children of Abraham. At the most basic level is the Christian dependence on the writings of the Tanakh. But since religious traditions are not static, but always in formation, Christians must also acknowledge other influences on our understanding of God along the way, from the vibrant medieval interdependen-

17. Walzer, *Thick and Thin,* p. 6.
18. David F. Ford, "Faith in the Third Millennium: Reading Scriptures Together," address at the Inauguration of Dr. Iain Torrance as President of Princeton Theological Seminary and Professor of Patristics, Thursday, March 10, 2005. This address and other writings on Scriptural Reasoning are available at http://etext.lib.virginia.edu/journals/jsrforum/writings.html.

cies among Jewish, Christian, and Muslim theologians, to twentieth-century European Christian efforts to unlearn "teachings of contempt" towards Judaism, to the theological commonalities that contemporary Christian churches in the global south find and cultivate with classical Islam. Every constructive interfaith conversation among Jews, Christians, and Muslims is an occasion for their mutual theological indebtedness to grow. As Wittgenstein would say, each conversation is an opportunity for them to come to think the same by learning more from each other about the God they worship.

God Between Christians and Jews:
Is It the Same God?

Alon Goshen-Gottstein

One possible starting point for an exploration of whether Jews and Christians believe in the same God is actually by examining different Jewish understandings of God. The fact is that there is no single Jewish understanding of God. Different periods and different schools have thought of God and approached Him in various ways. This diversity is an important resource for developing a Jewish approach to the Christian God. In part, certain views found within various strands of the Jewish tradition help narrow the gap between what might otherwise seem like completely incompatible views of God. From another perspective, the very diversity of Jewish views of God points to theological flexibility and accommodation. Differing views of God can coexist, with an implied understanding that it is the same God to which the various approaches point, despite their obvious differences. If such theological flexibility exists, why cannot the Christian God be recognized as one further expression of a Jewish approach to God? This is precisely where the "same-God" issue becomes the subject of discussion. Has the Christian view of God moved beyond the pale of Jewish theological flexibility, thereby making the Christian God an "other god," or can Judaism recognize that Christians worship the same God, despite whatever theological differences exist?

Judaism's only "statement" on Christianity provides us with a convenient way to begin our exploration. *Dabru Emet* is a statement on Christianity, published in the year 2000, by a team of Jewish scholars, in response to ongoing changes in the Christian churches in relation to

Judaism. It is an attempt to reciprocate various Christian statements on Jews and Judaism and is the first and only such attempt. The opening clause of *Dabru Emet* states: "Jews and Christians worship the same God." The description of Judaism and Christianity as worshiping the same God is disarmingly deceptive in its simplicity. Certainly to a Christian audience the point is obvious enough. Christian espousal of the Hebrew Bible leads naturally to the understanding that both parts of the Christian canon refer to the same God, even if what is known of God may have developed from one testament to the other. However, from a Jewish perspective this position is not self-evident. Indeed, for this reason the statement was included in *Dabru Emet,* and featured as its opening proposition. It is a position that must be constructed, rather than simply presented as a given of the Jewish attitude to Christianity. What follows is an attempt to explore and reveal some of the assumptions and choices involved in making *Dabru Emet's* opening proposition.

Recognizing the Same God: The Problem of *Avoda Zara*

The same-God discussion is a novel discussion. For most of Jewish history Jews either knew (or assumed) that their God was different from the gods of other people, or recognized that another religion worships God. While such recognition was rarely formulated in terms of the "same God," the question is actually the flipside of the foundational biblical perspective, forbidding the worship of other gods. "Other gods" is how the ten commandments refer to gods of other religions. In a polytheistic or henotheistic context, reference to other gods is self-evident, and the issue of "same God" does not even arise. It requires further theological evolution, and the clear recognition of a single divine presence, to raise the question of the same God.

The same-God discussion remains implicit in the formative stages of Jewish literature. The biblical reference to other gods gave way to another way of conceptualizing relations with other religions, developed in the rabbinic period. The rabbinic formulation, by means of which attitudes to other religions and their gods have been established, is in terms of the status of those religions as *Avoda Zara*. *Avoda Zara* is the formative category by means of which rabbinic literature assesses its attitudes to other religions and forms of worship. Literally the term means "foreign worship," designating the worship of foreign gods. While the term does not explicitly refer to idols, the objects of worship, but rather focuses upon the human act of worship, it is functionally equivalent to idolatry. The adequate translation of *Avoda Zara* lies somewhere between idolatry and false worship. Jewish tradition, and in particular the legal tradition, the halakha, which defines the contours of practical relations between Jews and people of other religions, has focused for the most part on the status of other religions as *Avoda Zara*. Framing the question in terms of *Avoda Zara* removes us one step from the same-God question, which was closer to the surface in the biblical formulation of "other gods." The present discussion will revisit the issue of *Avoda Zara* through the same-God lens, thereby bridging the gap between biblical and rabbinic formulations. It seeks to approach explicitly what for the most part remains implicit in both biblical and rabbinic approaches to other religions.

The present discussion focuses on the same-God question, from a Jewish perspective, in relation to Christianity. It allows us to tackle age-old questions from a fresh angle. Discussions of Christianity have taken place through the category of *Avoda Zara*. In examining these discussions in light of the same-God question, we may discover full or partial overlap between the issue of *Avoda Zara* and the same-God question. The same-God question can conceivably uncover the implicit assumptions of a discussion of *Avoda Zara*, provide a counterpoint to it, or redefine it, leading to novel views of *Avoda Zara* in light of the same-God question. It is thus a very helpful heuristic device, by means of which age-old questions of *Avoda Zara* may be revisited, appreciated anew, and possibly redefined. With reference to Christianity, the differences between alternative rabbinic positions could perhaps be accounted for in light of different views of the same-God question. Our choices between various options that the rabbinic tradition presents us with become clearer when these are viewed through the lens of the same-God question. It will therefore be helpful to enter the discussion of whether Judaism and Christianity worship the same God by revisiting the traditional Jewish formulation of the question of Christianity's status as *Avoda Zara*. In the process, we may expect a rich dialectic. The same-God discussion will be informed by the discussion of *Avoda Zara*, while at the same time it could provide new perspectives, which could in turn redefine the concept or the practical applications of *Avoda Zara* in relation to Christianity.

In traditional Jewish literature, expressed in the halakha, the governing question was whether Christianity is to be considered *Avoda Zara*. During the formative early rabbinic period, when the key concepts defining *Avoda Zara* were developed, Christianity was not yet one of the other religions, the validity of which Judaism had to assess in these terms. The consideration of Christianity in these rabbinic terms was primarily the work of halakhic authorities of the Middle Ages. The decision as to whether Christianity should or should not be considered *Avoda Zara* would have far-reaching ramifications on the daily life of Jews in Christian society. If Christianity was considered *Avoda Zara*, the strict application of talmudic law concerning commerce with idolaters would effectively preclude any possibility of commerce, hence of making a livelihood, in a Christian milieu. The definition of Christianity in this context was thus not a purely theological matter, but also a matter of developing strategies for Jewish survival.

The question of the halakhic status of Christianity, in terms of *Avoda Zara,* is twofold. Strictly speaking, what is under discussion is whether a Trinitarian understanding of God constitutes the kind of theological error that would lead to considering Christianity as *Avoda Zara.* In addition, Christian use of images in worship plays significantly into the question, informing both attitudes and positions vis-à-vis Christianity. The outward resemblance of forms of Christian worship and forms of worship typical of biblical and rabbinic idolatry enhances the perception of Christianity as *Avoda Zara.*

There is no single unequivocal position regarding Judaism's view of Christianity in terms of *Avoda Zara.* A range of possibilities was formulated throughout Judaism's rich history of contact with Christianity. This range is reflected in the diversity of halakhic approaches to Christianity down to present times. Clearly, the establishment of the state of Israel and the need to determine fundamental issues pertaining to other religions should have been the occasion for a systematic formulation of Judaism's attitude to other religions, including Christianity. Such a challenge has not been met in more than half a century of renewed Jewish life in Israel. A serious systematic reexamination of the topic, in light of a range of considerations — historical, sociological, and theological — seems overdue.

Positions on the question of the halakhic definition of Christianity as *Avoda Zara* diverge. Maimonides is the classical point of reference for considering Christianity as *Avoda Zara.* His enormous prestige, coupled at times with distance and lack of direct contact with Christianity, are among the factors for this position that often appears as the default Jewish position. An examination of contemporary rabbinic writings reveals how common the Maimonidean view of Christianity as *Avoda Zara* is, usually with little attention going into the matter, beyond the evocation of the Maimonidean position as self-evident.

Actually, it is far from clear what the reasoning for Maimonides' position on Christianity is. Maimonides offers this ruling in several places, but does not really attempt to explain the theological or other errors involved. Scholars are thus forced to conjecture what are the grounds for his declaration of Christianity as *Avoda Zara* and how these cohere with his broader worldview. Some scholars emphasize the philosophical/theological error involved in a Trinitarian view of the divinity. For Maimonides, "getting it right" theologically was of the utmost importance. Proper theological formulation was, for him, a condition for entry into the world to come. Hence the Maimonidean opposition to a range of theological misconceptions, assessed from the absolute vantage point of his philosophical worldview. This same worldview would be damning to many forms of Judaism, especially the kabbalistic tradition. That many of the halakhic authorities who adopt the Maimonidean view of Christianity also believe in Jewish doctrines that would not have received Maimonides' approval is testimony to the multiple forces that have shaped Jewish faith and halakha. In this case, positions were not shaped by the quest for theological consistency, as much as by the difference in attitude towards internal theological developments and the instinctive estrangement from the religion of the oppressive other.

If a wrong view of God is considered *Avoda Zara*, we may still be able to draw a distinction between the identity of God and the correct view of Him. Such a distinction would have particular power in the case of Maimonides, as it would apply equally to wrong Jewish views of God and to wrong non-Jewish notions. According to this reasoning, even if Christianity is considered *Avoda Zara* by the person who more than any other represents this position, this need not imply that Christians and Jews do not worship the same God.

My own reading of Maimonides, however, is different. In my view, the most likely reason for considering Christianity as *Avoda Zara* is that another being, other than God, is worshiped. For Maimonides, *Laws of Avoda Zara* 2:1, this is the core definition of *Avoda Zara*. This definition would put the same-God question right at the heart of discussion. If so, *Avoda Zara* and the same-God question would overlap, leading to the conclusion that the Christian God is another god.

However, even this conclusion may be overstated. For one, it may be a different God *in part*. As we shall see below, Maimonides may implicitly acknowledge the Christian knowledge of God is valid. If so, same-God and *Avoda Zara* operate under different premises. For a religion to be free of *Avoda Zara*, it must be *fully* clear of it. Such a high standard of expectation is commensurate with Maimonides' overall high theological standard. But even if it is not deemed "clear" or "clean" of *Avoda Zara*, it may nevertheless appeal to the same God. The same God may be known partially, while *Avoda Zara* requires full removal of theological or ritual imperfection. Returning to the affirmation of *Dabru Emet*, it may be that the sameness of the Christian and the Jewish God could be upheld even in spite of Maimonides' declaration of Christianity as *Avoda Zara*.

Other lines of reasoning could lead to a similar conclusion. *Avoda Zara* could be understood as an expression of wrong worship, a false approach to God. Such an understanding would obviously highlight inappropriate forms of worship — images, stones, or human beings. However, even if the form of worship is mistaken or forbidden, this need not impact on the identity of the God worshiped, only on the means by which He is worshiped. It is telling that when Maimonides narrates how *Avoda Zara* came into the world, in the first chapter of the *Laws of Avoda Zara*, he describes it as a function of a mistaken understanding of the will of God. Thus, God was worshiped in a wrong form, by giving honor to other beings. False worship can thus coexist with what is ultimately a correct identity of God. If so, we may legitimately distinguish the same-God question from the question of *Avoda Zara*.

Support for distinguishing between the two questions may be brought from Maimonides himself. In a famous responsum, Maimonides permits the teaching of Torah to Christians, while upholding the talmudic prohibition of teaching Torah to non-Jews in relation to Islam. The reason Maimonides offers is that Christians believe in the same revelation as we, and will therefore treat the Torah taught them respectfully, whereas Muslims do not show the same respect to our scriptures, claiming they have been falsified. Now, the acknowledgment of the validity of revelation is not simply a respectful attitude. It is a theological statement, involving a sense of who God is, the fact that He addresses us and what His revelation consists of. To claim that Christians recognize the same revelation as we and that their recognition is of halakhic consequence is also to make a statement concerning the faith that Christians have in the same revealing God. Maimonides' ruling is thus tantamount to recognition of a common faith in God in Judaism and Christianity.

The distinction between the question of *Avoda Zara* and the same-

God question is of great significance. On the face of it, if Christianity is considered *Avoda Zara,* this implies that Jews and Christians cannot speak of the same God. Indeed, one can trace in halakhic discourse that considers Christianity to be *Avoda Zara* the kind of distance and disdain that could not be entertained had the writers considered the Jewish God and the Christian God as one and the same. In terms of attitude, it is clear that the declaration of *Avoda Zara* and the sense of otherness in relation to the other religion's god do go hand in hand. Distinguishing between these two issues could open a space for recognition and respect for Christianity, even while upholding a variety of practical stringencies arising from the recognition that in technical and legal terms it is *Avoda Zara.* The possibility that Maimonides can be enlisted in support of such a distinction is particularly significant. If Maimonides conditions much of present-day halakhic attitudes to Christianity in ways that would seem to be negative and not supportive of respect and tolerance, the recognition that his rulings allow us to draw the distinction between the question of *Avoda Zara* and the same-God question is very significant for contemporary relations. Entering the discussion through the same-God portal significantly narrows the gap between Maimonides and the halakhic authorities we are about to discuss, who consider that it is permissible for non-Jews to worship God alongside other beings. From the perspective of *Avoda Zara* there is a radical difference between them, with the Maimonidean position leading to rejection of the legitimacy of Christianity. Seen, however, from the perspective of the same-God question, the gap between these positions may disappear. Both positions may be able to recognize that the God of Judaism and the God of Christianity are one and the same. Let us, then, turn to an examination of the position typically considered as the alternative to Maimonides'.

The position considered alternative to Maimonides' position was formed initially as a response to practical demands, arising out of the financial needs of Jews living in Christian lands. Over time it evolved into a principled position with regard to Christianity. The position, usually associated with the twelfth-century figure of Rabbenu Tam, considers the Christian God in terms of the rabbinic category of *Shituf,* association. One must not worship another being alongside God. However, argues Rabbenu Tam, the prohibition against *Shituf,* the worship of another being alongside God, applies only to Jews. Non-Jews are not prohibited from such worship. Therefore, the worship of another being, Jesus, alongside the biblical God, does not violate the norms by which non-Jews are expected to act, according to halakha. The upshot of this position is that restrictions that would apply had Christianity been considered *Avoda Zara* do not apply. Presumably, the underlying theological understanding is that compromising absolute monotheistic understanding of God is permitted to non-Jews, as long as one does not lose contact with the worship of the One God. Jews, by contrast, are commanded to a higher or stricter monotheistic norm, according to which no other being may be worshiped alongside God.

By the eighteenth century, the position that non-Jews are not prohibited from worshiping God in association with other beings had become a principled acceptance of Christianity as a valid religion. What started out as a mechanism for solving a specific legal problem involving financial transactions with Christians became a principled recognition of the legitimacy of Christianity. Christianity was religiously legitimate and was not considered as *Avoda Zara,* because Judaism could not fault the Christian understanding of God as valid for Christian believers. The move was a brilliant one. This position recognized the legitimacy of Christianity for non-Jews. For Jews, however, it was considered invalid, as they were prohibited from worshiping God alongside another being. Tolerance of the other and protection of one's own from the dangers of Christianity were thus achieved through the same theological move.

Contemporary rabbinic discussions oscillate between the positions of Maimonides and Rabbenu Tam. One of the problems for a contemporary Jewish view of the Christian God is the lack of a single considered Jewish position concerning the Christian God. Needless to say, the fundamental attitude to Christianity changes radically if it is considered *Avoda Zara* or not. As mentioned, one of the implications of considering Christianity as *Avoda Zara* is that a distance is kept from it, in practical as well as in theological, emotional, and other senses. This distance is not necessarily bridged if *Shituf* is considered permitted. Much depends on how the permissibility of *Shituf* is understood, on the one hand, and on the relationship of *Shituf* to the same-God question. *Shituf* may be understood either as nonidolatrous or as a form of idolatry permissible for non-Jews. Positions on these issues need not overlap and may be variously configured. One possible aligning of positions would be that if *Shituf* is not *Avoda Zara,* then indeed Jews and Christians do worship the same God, even if Christians understand that God differently. If so, *Shituf* refers to the means of approaching the same God. Jews and Christians differ in their use of means, but the end is the same. According to this way of parsing the question, *Avoda Zara* overlaps with the same-God question, and from both perspectives Christianity is viewed positively.

If we continue to align the positions, what of the understanding that *Shituf* is a form of permitted *Avoda Zara*? Declaring *Shituf* a form of *Avoda Zara* does not necessarily preclude recognition of the same God. After all, permissibility of *Shituf* is founded upon such recognition. If despite such recognition, Christianity is considered *Avoda Zara*, even if permissible for non-Jews, one would be forced to conclude that Christians worship the same God, but approach Him through the worship of others — an approach that even if permissible is not free of the taint of *Avoda Zara*. Accordingly, Jews and Christians could be said to worship the same God *in part*.

Because the question of *Avoda Zara* has not been explored classically through the lens of the same-God question, authorities who affirmed Christianity's legitimacy never framed its recognition in such partial terms. Nevertheless, the strategies for recognizing Christianity do appeal to same-God arguments, and they do so precisely *in part*, that is, by affirming certain aspects of the Christian recognition of God, rather than others. Legitimators of Christianity on the grounds of the permissibility of *Shituf* for non-Jews have to, in some way, emphasize the identity of the one God by highlighting certain features of the common understanding of God, at the expense of the particularly unique Christian doctrine. Thus, creation, providence, and revelation are some of the doctrines that are suggested as common theological ground, supporting faith in the same God. Let us look at how such affirmation is achieved in greater detail.

The rabbinic authorities that uphold the permissibility of *Shituf* and who recognize Christianity resort frequently to the same-God argument. While creation forms the basis for the same-God argument, it does get expanded in later iterations. The following famed passage from the seventeenth-century Rabbi Moshe Rivkes makes the point:

> What the talmudic rabbis state, in this matter, was only said with reference to the gentiles who were in their own times, who would worship stars and signs and who did not believe in the Exodus and in the creation of the world. But these non-Jews in whose shadow we the Israelite nation dwell and are spread amidst them, they believe in the creation of the world and the Exodus from Egypt and in the principles of faith, and their entire intention is to the maker of heaven and earth. . . . We are obligated to pray for their welfare. . . . David's prayer for God to pour His wrath on the nations who do not know Him (Ps. 79:6) refers

to the non-Jews who do not believe in the creation of the world and the matter of signs and miracles that God did with us in Egypt and in the giving of the Torah. But the nations in whose shadow we live and dwell under their wings, they believe in all these, and we continually pray for the[ir] peace.

This formulation yields several alternative definitions of how one recognizes the same God. God's creative power is surely the clearest distinguishing mark of God's identity. His power to do miracles, His intervention in history, His revelation are all divine identity markers. It may be that belief in a common Scripture itself points to the identity of the God in whom one believes. Thus, not only God's actions but the acceptance of the scriptures in which His deeds are narrated provide ways of identifying God. We shall return to this point shortly, when we revisit Maimonides' views.

Recognizing the same God, through common religious propositions and faith articles, is a matter of theological choice. Were one to highlight all that is strange, foreign, and unacceptable about Christian faith, one would have to forego recognition of the same God. What leads to affirmation rather than rejection of the same-God premise is more than the practical social and economic needs that mandate recognizing the two religions as serving the same God. Ultimately, it is the product of religious intuition, whereby religious affinity and commonality are recognized and by means of which the identity of God in both traditions is affirmed. However, this intuition does not stand on its own. Considering this intuition independently might lead us to conclude that Jews and Christians fully worship the same God. Rather, this intuition drives, and in part complements, a conceptual construct by means of which similarity and difference are simultaneously affirmed. *Shituf* may be indebted to a fundamental religious intuition, but its conceptual work is more complex than this religious intuition. Built into this category is the possibility for affirming similarity and otherness, depending on how one wishes to apply it. It thus calls for a choice, of whether the God of Judaism and the God of Christianity are one, and for clear articulation of the theological criteria by means of which such a choice is made.

Recognizing the Same God: Worship and Story

A consideration of Christianity's status as *Avoda Zara* cannot exhaust the question of the identity of the Jewish and Christian God. Halakhic discussion leaves the question at hand undecided. Due to the historical exigencies and circumstances of how halakhic positions were formulated it may also not offer us the most balanced approach to the question, reflecting as it does more the history of internal Jewish legal thinking than a direct theological assessment of Christianity.

Underlying the discussion of the identity of the God of Judaism and the God of Christianity is a weighty philosophical challenge: recognizing the God of other religions as identical to or as different from the God in whom we (in this instance: as Jews) believe. The discussion above of Christianity's status as *Avoda Zara* relied heavily upon a theological approach to the problem. Maimonides' position has been understood by some readers as based on his philosophical understanding of the problematics of the Trinity, while adherents of the permissibility of *Shituf* appealed to common theological statements, by means of which the identity of God, as known in both religions, could be established. As suggested above, taking the theological route in order to establish that the same God is worshiped in both religions involves us in selectivity and overlooking certain portions of the faith of the other, while highlighting others.

That the halakhic process and its theologizing may yield conflicting results, as our previous discussion indicates, is in part a consequence of the historical and sociological circumstances that gave birth to the various positions of rabbinic authorities. It is, however, also an indication of the problem of establishing the identity of God by means of the halakhic process and particularly through its appeal to philosophical or theological arguments. Halakhico-theological analysis is inconclusive because more is involved in religion than theological pronouncements on the nature of God. Proof for this may be found in an examination of halakhic attitudes to Islam. Despite the fact that Islam does not raise the same theological difficulties in its understanding of the unity of God that Christianity does, various rabbinic authorities consider it nevertheless to be *Avoda Zara*. This significant minority rabbinic position points to the choices involved in viewing another religion. Highlighting particular aspects of a religion may lead to its consideration as *Avoda Zara*, even if its concept of God is not faulted. Thus, more is involved in the declaration of another religion as *Avoda Zara* than pure theology. A statement that another religion is *Avoda Zara* is more than a theological statement about the nature of the god of another religion. It involves issues of otherness and identity of the religious community, as well as other sociological, cultural, and historical considerations. The identity of God in different religions — the same-God question — is thus related to some extent to considerations of the identity of the religious community in relation to other communities. If this is acknowledged, at least in some cases, then it is clear that more than theology is involved in establishing the identity of God in two religions. The identity of God in different religions can be established only in part through the theological statements made of Him, the attributes assigned to Him, and the names by which He is known. In the case of Judaism and Christianity we find alongside similarities also differences in each of these categories.

The nature of the choice involved in establishing the identity of God between religions will become more obvious when we consider the problem of identity of God within the religion — in our case, Judaism. As already stated, there are significant theological differences in the understanding of God between different schools in Judaism. From a strictly substantive or theological perspective, these differences are no less significant than the differences between Judaism and Christianity. However, despite the internal differences between kabbalists and philosophers, we do not find within internal Jewish debates, to the best of my awareness, the charge that a different God is being worshiped, or that one side or the other is guilty of *Avoda Zara*. This leads us to conclude that more is involved in the establishment of the identity or difference of God in different religions than the working out of theological issues; it leads us to a consideration of the means by which God is recognized and acknowledged within Jewish tradition.

A discussion of God in Judaism is inextricably linked with a discussion of ritual and of history. The covenant provides the logic for Israel's story and the framework for worship, from within which God is recognized and approached. Different approaches to God, characteristic of the different periods and schools of Judaism, share in a common story and provide different understandings of a common ritual. The centrality of story and worship is expressed in the ritual of conversion to Judaism. Significantly, the conversion ritual by means of which one enters Judaism lacks theological emphasis. The potential convert affirms his or her desire to become part of the people and their commitment to follow the commandments. These are the primary criteria for joining the Jewish people. Story (entry into the people) and ritual (acceptance of the yoke of the commandments) define Jewish identity, rather than theological affirmation. Even though the theological differences between different schools of kabbalists and philosophers may be as significant as the differences between Jewish and Christian teachings of God, the wider context within which these differences are articulated is more significant than the differences themselves. The most appropriate reply to the question, Who is the God of Israel? would thus be: the God who is known through Israel's story and through its worship.

Significantly, as Rabbi Yehuda Halevi has already pointed out, the ten commandments open with the identification of God as the God who took Israel out of Egypt, rather than as the God who created heaven and earth. Story (Israel's redeemer) rather than an attribute (God as creator) provides God's identity. It is the God who liberated Israel from Egypt, who entered a covenantal relation with them, and who continues to be involved in their story. It is the God who commanded a way of life, and who is known and approached through the commandments He gave His people. All theological speculations and definitions are secondary to this primary mode of recognizing God. God is known through relationship and action, and they provide the stability of identity as well as continuity to the diverse forms of historical Judaism. The ultimate reason why various Jewish approaches to God can agree upon the identity of the God they worship, and hence recognize each other as members of the same religion, is that Judaism is not constituted through theological definition. Rabbinic Judaism, philosophical Judaism, and the various strands of kabbalistic Judaism share a common worship. The identity of the God of Judaism is established through this common worship more than through any of the theological statements made by these different Judaisms.

If story and worship establish the identity of the God who is at the center of a religion, the question of the relationship of the God of Judaism and the God of Christianity takes on new dimensions. Instead of a consideration of the relative significance of specific theological proclamations in the overall economy of the religion — God the creator of heaven and earth versus the triune God — the continuity, or lack thereof, between the Jewish and Christian stories and forms of worship will be the focus of attention. Such a focus not only serves as an important complement and corrective to the classical theological emphasis; it is also truer to the historical causes of the divide between Judaism and Christianity. Judaism and Christianity did not divide over the appropriate understanding of God. The separation between the two religions occurred over two issues — the definition of "Israel," and the continued relevance of the commandments. How "Israel" is defined touches upon the heart of Israel's story and determines what will be considered the next chapter in this ongoing story. Abandonment of the commandments amounts to a change of the entire religious structure, hence the creation of a new religion. If a common worship allows us to recognize diverse theological forms of Judaism as pointing to the same God, the lack of such common form of worship ultimately raises the question of the identity of the God of Judaism and the God of Christianity.

I am convinced that had Judaism and Christianity not parted ways, yielding different religions between which no love was lost, a particular understanding of God, such as the Trinitarian understanding, could have been recognized as part of a wide range of acceptable Jewish understandings of and approaches to God. Had the faith of Christianity remained true to classical Jewish ritual expression, there would have been little question as to the identity of God being worshiped through this ritual, even if a particular understanding of this God characterized a specific community of believers. Historical research suggests a far greater diversity in the understanding of the one God in late antiquity than is often recognized. Christian understanding could have conceivably developed as one form of Jewish understanding.

This suggestion can be considered not only from the perspective of Judaism in late antiquity, but also from the perspective of the Judaism of the Middle Ages. In and of itself, the understanding of the triune God, as taught by Christianity, is no more or less acceptable than the teaching of the decaune God — God as manifest through the tenfold *sefirotic* structure, as taught by the Kabbalah. Kabbalah was accepted, not because of the inherent appeal or conviction of its teachings, but because of the enormous prestige of the rabbinic authorities who supported and taught it, when it became a historical phenomenon. In other words, beyond the specific teaching lies the wider religious context. The difficulty in the Christian theological position — hence, in the recognition of the Christian God as the same as the God of Judaism — is not exclusively a function of the position itself. It is no less a consequence of the wider context of separation, competition, rejection, and hate, in sum: the difference through which the two religions assess each other.

If the context determines as much, perhaps more than theology itself, let us consider the two primary modes of establishing the context of reflection on God — story and ritual, as they impact the question of the identity of the Jewish and Christian God. I begin with ritual and then move on to some thoughts on the commonality of story. The suggestion that God's identity is established through worship, or perhaps better, through the theological recognition captured in worship, rather than through theological statements, may allow us to approach the question of the identity of the God of Judaism and the God of Christianity from a novel angle. As with the theological approach to the issue, there are multiple perspectives from which the question can be addressed. On the face of it, Christian worship is distinct from Jewish worship. Christianity rejected the Jewish observance of the mitzvot and instituted its own rituals and sacraments, principal among which is the celebration of the Eucharist. On the face of it, then, shifting the ground of discussion from theological doctrine to the common ground of worship is of little help. It would seem that the difference in practice actually increases the sense of difference between the religions, thereby enhancing the sense of otherness, both of Christianity and its God.

While Christian worship has taken on a very different quality from Jewish worship, one may nevertheless point to significant elements of Christian worship that point to the identity of the God that is worshiped with the God of Judaism. Unlike proper theological understanding, regarding which one may argue that imperfect theological understanding may be construed as *Avoda Zara* and hence hamper the recognition of the same God worshiped in both religions, the perspective of worship need not seek full compatibility of worship and its implicit theology. If worship is used to indicate the identity of the God who is worshiped, His identity may be established even if details of worship reflect theological differences. The theological perspective tends to be maximalist, seeking full or significant accord concerning how God is understood. Worship, by contrast, may provide a more minimalist position, seeking to find sufficient common ground in worship to point to the identity of the God approached in Judaism and Christianity.

Despite great differences in Jewish and Christian worship, there are some significant commonalities in their form of worship. Christians often appeal to the commonality in prayer, suggested by the fact that both Jews and Christians express their prayers through the Psalms. Indeed, the Psalms provide Jews and Christians with a common language and text of prayer. If the Psalms alone were considered, one might conclude that this common form of worship does indeed point to a common referent of worship, the one God.

The argument from common worship might be profitably expanded to include not only the Psalms, but the entire Hebrew Bible, acknowledged as part of Christian Scripture. One may argue that the identity of God is established not only through the medium of a common text that addresses God in prayer, but also through the common text, God's word common to both traditions. Accordingly, the fact that both Judaism and Christianity recognize the Bible might allow us to propose a new way of establishing the identity of God in both religions. Both religions recognize the God of the Hebrew Bible. If Jews and Christians share Scripture, they share something fundamental also in the identity of the God who expresses Himself through this same Scripture. This brings us back to the responsum of Maimonides, discussed above. The recognition of shared Scripture between Jews and Christians is deemed religiously significant by Maimonides, and ultimately functions as a same-God strategy. As suggested above, Maimonides' use of this strategy should be appreciated against the background of his ruling that Christianity is *Avoda Zara*. If that decision was reached on account of Christian theological views, then we can see clearly where different criteria would lead to different approaches to Christianity. Theological criteria would lead to proclamation of Christianity as *Avoda Zara,* while the criteria of worship, and possibly story, as these are expressed through common Scripture, allow us to recognize the same God in Judaism and Christianity.

Applying the criterion of common worship as a means of recognizing the same God could be seen as counterintuitive. While elements of worship that are common to Jews and Christians are offered to God, Christian worship is explicitly addressed to Jesus, as God. Larry Hurtado makes us aware of worship as the decisive moment where legitimate theological diversity turns into religious otherness. The common worship strategy therefore requires a good deal of theological will. Theological minimalism requires not only establishing minimal criteria for recognizing the same God through worship, but also putting aside significant theological differences, as these concern the explicit object of worship.

Returning to Scripture, it can be thought of also as an expression of story. Scripture provides Israel's formative story. Sharing Scripture therefore poses the question of whether there is a way of sharing in Israel's story that might be incorporated into a same-God strategy for recognizing Christianity. God would thus be known as the same God because He is the God of the same unfolding story, the story of Abraham, Isaac, Jacob, and Israel, known through the Bible and commonly professed by Jews and Christians. One recalls Pascal's famous proclamation of faith — "Fire. God of Abraham, God of Isaac, God of Jacob, not of the philosophers and the scholars." Rabbi Yehuda Halevy would have been fully sympathetic to this ascription of God. Pascal here juxtaposes a philosophical or theological means of knowing God with the way in which God is known directly, through an unfolding story. Thus, recognizing the common scriptural foundations of Judaism and Christianity opens the gate to the recognition of the same God, known from a common story.

In purely theoretical terms, this may be the most effective way of establishing the identity of the God of Judaism and the God of Christianity. It is, however, also the most emotionally charged path and one that could meet with considerable resistance. The reason for this does not lie in the argument itself, but in the broader context of how the stories of Judaism and Christianity have been told for millennia. For the better part of the history of Jewish-Christian relations, Christians have told the biblical story at the expense of Jews. Their identification with the biblical story was made possible, for the most part, by displacing Israel and taking their place in the story. Christians could recognize the God of Abraham, Isaac, and Jacob because they had become the true Israel.

For Jews to recognize the God of Christians as their own because of a common story touches on the heart of the Jewish-Christian divide. It is emotionally charged, but also has great theological potential. The past decades have seen a reversal of Christian theology, in most major denominations, leading to a recognition of the enduring value of Israel's relationship with God and its particular story. This breakthrough brings a same-story approach to the same-God problem into the realm of the possible. However, Christian theology has a long way to go in reconciling its own identity as Israel with the enduring identity of the people of Israel as the people of the covenant. Formative declarations such as *Nostra Aetate* pave the way for important theological work that has yet to take place. It may therefore take time for a same-story strategy to mature, in ways that do not make the Jewish side uncomfortable. From a Jewish perspective, recognizing common Scripture as the foundation for a common story requires developing a broader theological understanding of the role of Christianity within the divine economy and for how it relates to Judaism's ultimate purpose. This theological line of thinking requires much work. Recognizing a common God through story is best achieved by appeal to the initial common foundations of the story. To look at the foundations of the story while disregarding its continuation is clearly problematic and involves a conscious turning away from most of Judaism's history with Christianity. Such a strategy therefore requires further theological thinking and advances on both the Jewish and the Christian side.

While the full impact of this strategy may become visible only in the future, it is important to recognize that we possess several precedents for considering Christianity in terms of Judaism's own story. The same

Maimonides who recognizes the religious value of common Scripture in relation to Christianity also offers a reading of history in which the global spreading of Christianity paves the way for the ultimate recognition of truth, in messianic times, through the sharing of biblical language, story, and concepts. Maimonides does not make the same-God argument explicitly, but it is implicit in the recognition of the same story. The same is true for another telling of the Christian story from Jewish eyes. Rabbi Yakov Emden incorporates the story of Jesus and Paul within the Jewish narrative, by presenting them as teachers of the seven Noachide commandments, who sought to bring this instruction to all of humanity. Unlike Maimonides, Emden did not consider Christianity to be *Avoda Zara*. If Jesus was a Jewish teacher and Christianity fulfills the obligations of the Noachide commandments, the same-God issue does not even arise; it is taken for granted.

These two rabbinic authors show that Christianity's story can be incorporated within Judaism's. When such incorporation is coupled with explicit Christian appeal to the common roots of the story, it makes the same-story argument as a means for establishing the identity of God credible. The constructs of Emden and Maimonides were meant for internal Jewish purposes and were composed under certain historical conditions. Changes in historical conditions, and in particular in Christian views of Judaism, raise new challenges with regard to the possibility of incorporating Christianity within Israel's story. While meeting those challenges may require time, it is promising that one of the most effective strategies for recognizing the same God has such precedent within Jewish tradition.

The preceding discussion attempted to suggest certain criteria for recognizing the same God. These criteria are often found alongside the theological criteria, discussed earlier in this paper. In fact, they provide independent tracks to addressing the question. Our discussion suggests that much like the theological criteria themselves, applying these criteria as a means of recognizing the same God requires prior theological will, and relies on intuition and recognition. The appeal to both worship and story does not provide unequivocal proof. Rather, it functions as a way of constructing an argument, for which prior motivation must exist. In my view, the more effective argument is the argument from the same story, an argument that sidesteps theology and that relies on precedent. However, even this argument cannot be taken for granted. It expresses prior attitudes, and may therefore be suitable for those who wish to affirm the same God in both traditions, within the present theological and sociological climate.

Still, like all other arguments, it must be constructed. Its contemporary construction constitutes an invitation to continuing theological reflection concerning Judaism's and Christianity's common story.

Recognizing the Same God: Morality and Spiritual Life

The challenge of recognizing the same God behind different religious traditions is wider than the challenge posed within the framework of Jewish-Christian relations. Emphasis upon common worship and common story is appropriate to Judaism's consideration of Christianity, in view of the particular relationship between the two religions. The following consideration is potentially appropriate to all religious traditions, even though it was articulated historically in relation to Christianity. In dealing with the status of Christianity, as well as Islam, from a Jewish perspective, a novel and principled position was marshaled by the fourteenth-century Provençal Rabbi Menachem HaMeiri.

Let me introduce Meiri by considering Judaism's attitude to other religions in historical context. This is particularly important for the present focus on the same-God question. The biblical references to other gods and the talmudic references to *Avoda Zara* create a culture of distance and disdain in relation to other religions. This attitude, formulated in response to the religions of antiquity and late antiquity, was, on the whole, transferred into the Middle Ages, and conditioned Jewish attitudes towards Christianity. However, Christianity, as well as Islam, presented challenges that are unique in the history of Jewish dealings with other religions, both theologically and sociologically. Theologically, no longer was one dealing with other gods, but with other *religions* that claimed to worship the same God. For the modern observer who encounters Jewish attitudes to other religions, it is often difficult to understand on what grounds Jews could reject either religion, claiming they are *Avoda Zara,* given that they basically believe in the same God. Carrying over the charge of *Avoda Zara* from classical literature to the dealings with Christianity, and even with Islam, is part of the heritage of Judaism, as it confronts new religious forms while preserving the categories and attitudes of old. That such continuity should exist is in part an expression of Jewish faithfulness and fidelity. It is, as already suggested above, also a consequence of the adoption of methods of worship, through image and form, that evoke a deep sense of otherness, coupled with a theology that is hard to reconcile with classical Jewish views of God. Finally, it cannot be divorced from the historical and socio-logical reality of Jews living as a minority, often a persecuted minority, in Christian and Muslim lands. Such historical conditions do not easily lend themselves to profound theological rethinking of one's attitude to the op-pressive majority society. All these factors conspire to maintain age-old at-titudes to other religions and to their application to Christianity.

Meiri is to be appreciated within this context. Over and against the various halakhic authorities who resolved challenges in day-to-day living in relation to Christians and Christianity on an ad hoc basis, Meiri devel-oped a systematic view of other religions and in fact constituted one of the earliest attempts to formulate a broad Jewish theology of contemporary religions. One way of stating Meiri's achievement is to present him as hav-ing moved from framing the broader issues in terms of *Avoda Zara* to thinking of them in terms of the same God. Systematic application of this perspective yields a systemic revolution in relation to contemporary reli-gions. It is beyond the scope of the present paper to present the various implications of Meiri's revolution to Judaism's attitudes to world religions. For present purposes two points are crucial. The first is that Meiri is the one and only halakhist who resolves the question of *Avoda Zara* fully and exclusively by using a same-God strategy. Having recognized that the God of Judaism and the God of other contemporary religions are one, the way was opened for him to declare all talmudic issues pertaining to *Avoda Zara* as no longer valid for contemporary religions. Application of *Avoda Zara* would seem impossible, once it is recognized that two religions worship the same God. *Avoda Zara* would thus be understood, following biblical foundations, as worship of another God rather than as the entry into the domain of otherness, be it the otherness of other people, other religions, or other practices and ways of worship. For Meiri, therefore, there is no ques-tion that the God of Christianity and the God of Judaism are one.

This leads to the second important point in our discussion: What is the method by means of which Meiri arrives at this recognition? Here we find another way of approaching the same-God question and indeed an important theoretical contribution to any same-God discussion. In order to appreciate it we need to look more closely at Meiri's reasoning. Meiri's views are summed up by two main claims. The first concerns the nature of idolatry of old, presumably biblical and rabbinic, and its relation to con-temporary religions. According to Meiri, idolatry of old no longer exists, except in remote regions. Accordingly, all that appears in talmudic sources concerning pagans and idol worshipers is no longer relevant to contemporary religions. As Moshe Halbertal has suggested, Meiri relies on a theory of religious progress. *Avoda Zara* is really a matter of the past, as humanity and its religions have progressed from earlier primitive (fetishist) understanding, to a higher understanding of God. Such a theory of progress draws from philosophical literature of the Middle Ages, but it seems to me it draws no less on the fundamental distinction between the religions of old and the religions that Meiri encounters. Here intuition may be at play again. To the theoretical discussion may be added the intuitive understanding that one's neighbors or conversation partners are not the base idolaters described in the Talmud. Meiri shares a common universe of discourse with Christian scholars. We know of intellectual exchanges between himself and Christian clergy, and his entire spiritual environment is one in which the intellectuals and thinkers of the different religions form bonds of common community and purpose. Such a climate of sharing provides a counterpoint to prevailing attitudes of Jewish minorities in other European centers and may be one of the factors that allow Meiri's attitudes to flourish. Within this context one can readily consider the view of progress in the history of religions, according to which the religions seen today — notably Christianity and Islam in Meiri's case — are fundamentally different from the religions spoken of in the Talmud. As a consequence, many of the talmudic rulings concerning *Avoda Zara* no longer apply.

The other key component in Meiri's view is the recognition that the nations of today are bound by moral codes and practice moral living. Meiri uses the moral argument to distinguish between the religions of old and contemporary religions. Today's nations are restricted by the ways of religion. They possess a moral code. The negative and immoral representations of non-Jews found in earlier sources therefore do not apply to them.

A key challenge in understanding Meiri is to understand the relation between the two components of Meiri's thought. What is the relation between the claim that contemporary religions are not idolatrous and their description as moral and law-abiding? On first view, Meiri shifts the ground of discussion from theology — the ground upon which most considerations of Christianity's status as *Avoda Zara* took place — to morality. Rather than focus upon the nature of the understanding of the Divine espoused by a given religion, Meiri claims the relevant consideration is the moral life enabled by the religion. Religions that have a moral code should not be considered along the lines the Talmud prescribes for idolatrous religions. However, upon closer examination, Meiri's position should be understood not as an avoidance of the theological dimension, but as establishing a different method by means of which the identity of the God worshiped by a religion may be known. Accordingly, the life of the believers, rather than the theological statements of the religion, is the ultimate proof of identity of its God. A religion that teaches and upholds a moral way of living is proof of the God who is worshiped through that religion. We may thus posit the following understanding of the relationship between Meiri's two statements regarding contemporary religions. The second statement, according to which the nations of today are bound by the boundaries of religion, holds the key to the first — that they are no longer idolatrous. It is not simply that they have ceased to worship idols, but rather that the means by which we are able to make this statement is through an examination of the moral quality of their lives. Morality points to the God who is known through the religion, and moral living suggests a notion of God that is real, in terms of His impact upon the lives of believers.

Meiri does not overlook the diversity of religious practice, ritual, and specific beliefs about God that distinguish different religions. Still, he is willing to consider them all as legitimate forms of religion. This assumes an ability to distinguish what is fundamental to a religion from what is secondary or instrumental. I would not say that for Meiri all of religion is simply a means of establishing a moral society. Rather, religion is about transforming the human person towards a higher spiritual vision associated with God. Details of theology are secondary to the approach to God. The same holds true for variations of ritual practice.

Meiri's structure drives home an important lesson for the same-God discussion. There is no God of this and God of that religion. There is only God. Therefore, a religion, a lifestyle, or a set of practices either does bring one into relationship with God, or it doesn't. The core question is thus even more fundamental than the same-God question — it is simply the "God question." Once it is recognized that a given religion provides access to God, all other details are secondary.

Meiri is revolutionary in how he formulates the question, in the method he adopts for answering it, and in the conclusions — both theological and practical — that he reaches. Informing his entire approach is the recognition that God is known through the ethical lives of believers. In what follows, I would like to extend this criterion from the ethical lives of believers to the overall spiritual lives of believers, as a way of further advancing our discussion of the same-God question — or perhaps, following Meiri, we ought to simply say "the God question." Applying the moral test to the question of the identity of the God worshiped in a religion assumes

God can be known through the fruits of contact with Him or with the teachings communicated in His name. This principle can be extended from basic morality to other aspects of the spiritual life. We may consider the effects of contact with God upon the human person as indications of the identity of God. These can include those expressions of moral and spiritual excellence that constitute religious perfection: humility, service, loving-kindness, compassion, etc. Meiri's principle may be further extended to formative experiences of God, as these register within human awareness and as they shape the religious personality. Recognizing God through the traces of contact left in His human relationship partners may serve as an alternative to theological formulations that attempt to define or proclaim the nature of God. If so, lives are testimonies to God and God's friends, and those who live in His presence are the proof of His existence as well as identity.

This position has serious consequences for the very possibility of juxtaposing, contrasting, and demarcating religions in absolute ways. The serious implications of such a position are that true and false knowledge of God are no longer the demarcating lines distinguishing between my religion and the religion of the other. Instead, true and false knowledge, true worship, and idolatrous appeal to religion are inherent in all religions. Validity and value are not givens of any religion, its doctrine, or its practices. They are no less a function of the degree to which any religion forms a true attachment to God.

If we can consider God not through teaching, story, and philosophical formulation, but through the living traces of His presence, as these are made known in the lives of believers, this permits a fresh consideration of the question of the God of Judaism and the God of Christianity. Certainly, there has been much in the history of Christianity, especially as this concerns its relations with Judaism, that has not been worthy of association with God, and that could therefore be labeled as the imprint of other gods within the Christian religion. Yet, other sections of Christianity do witness the living presence of God. I think of the lives of the outstanding Christian saints, whose teaching, example, and inspiration are among the finest fruits of the human spirit and constitute signs of how God touches the lives and hearts of humans. I think of the religious teachings, moral as well as spiritual, that indicate direct awareness of God and His ways. I think even of the power of repentance and transformation that have characterized major denominations of contemporary Christianity in their relationship with Judaism. These are all fruits of a living spirit that offers testimony to God.

To think of recognition of the God of Christianity through the lives of Christian believers makes us confront simultaneously the worst, as well as the best, in Christianity. The finest examples of spiritual lives are contrasted with ugly moments from the history of Jewish-Christian relations. We are, however, at a point in time at which Christians have confronted their own past. This confrontation has been understood by Christians as an expression of the Holy Spirit in their lives, leading them to *teshuva* (metanoia). As we have come to learn at every point in our reflections on the God of Judaism and Christianity, there comes a point of choice. Here too we have the choice of recognizing this repentance, and opening ourselves to the recognition of God, as He has been known in the lives of believing Christians, notwithstanding the moments of darkness that have shaped so much of Judaism's encounter with Christianity.

Shifting the testing ground for religious authenticity and for the identity of God from theology to human behavior and experience has a corollary in the attitude that religions would adopt to one another. Testimony and listening would replace philosophical argument and interreligious debate. Recognizing God's presence and reality in the life and religion of the other constitutes a testimony to God that transcends differences in names of God and in forms of religious life. Rather than assuming that a religion — any religion — does or does not appeal to the one God, the true God, the correct God — our God — we should seek traces of the one living God where these are found.

Conclusion: God in Judaism and Christianity — Awaiting the Future

In examining the Christian God from a Jewish perspective we posed two questions. One was whether the Jewish God and the Christian God are one and the same. The second was whether the Christian view of God could be considered as one more expression of a great variety of Jewish understandings of God. It seems to me that both questions require awaiting the future, rather than focusing exclusive attention on historical formulations of Judaism and Christianity. Historical precedent presented us with a variety of positions. As noted, contemporary Judaism has not come to an unequivocal position in its view of the Christian God. Recognizing the identity of the Christian God therefore remains an act of choice, whether it is a choice between existing rabbinic options or the choice needed in order to construct a given theological position, as various such points of choice have emerged in the framework of this paper.

As concerns the question of the legitimacy of a Trinitarian understanding of God from a Jewish perspective, this too is not a matter that one may pose in a historical vacuum. There is, interestingly enough, some historical precedent for a Jewish recognition of the validity of certain ways of understanding the Christian Trinity. However, this is uncharacteristic of Jewish attitudes to Christianity. Most of the Jewish attitude to Christian doctrine is conditioned by the historical circumstances that highlight the difference between the religions, enforcing the sense that Christianity is the religion of the other. From such a perspective it makes little sense to ask why Christian understanding could not be considered one more form of legitimate Jewish belief. The reason is perhaps not inherent in the belief itself, as much as in the fact that the belief defined the identity of a religious other. History cannot be undone. We can only look to the next chapter of the story, where we may find the hope for a different and better future. Whether that future might allow for a deeper theological rapprochement between the traditions is a matter upon which one can only speculate.

In concluding this essay, I would like to return to the strategy that seems to me personally to hold the greatest value in and of itself and the greatest promise for leading us towards a better and more spiritual future, a future that holds great hope for Jewish-Christian relations, as well as for interfaith relations in general. The path that I would personally give greatest weight to is the path that recognizes God not through doctrine, but through the signs of God's presence in the lives of the faithful. Such recognition calls for a different kind of listening and attention to the spiritual reality of Christianity than has been characteristic of Judaism for all of its history. I believe the future mandates a different kind of listening, as part of a quest that must be undertaken by all religions to find the traces of the living God in all religions.

The suggestion that God's identity may be established through traces of His presence in the lives of believers seems to me particularly interesting. I, and many others, consider Judaism to be in crisis. At the heart of that crisis, as I have argued elsewhere, is the crisis of God. While God remains the conceptual center of Judaism, His presence is usually eclipsed by other values that govern Jewish life — the Jewish people, Torah study, the land, and even faithfulness to God. This has been felt most keenly by the droves of Jewish youth who flock to India, many in search of a spiritual life they did not find in Judaism. The search for God, when extended to other religions, has not led to renewed Jewish interest in Christianity. The reasons for this lie in history, not in theology. Recognizing the divine presence in the lives of believers is a powerful strategy for recognizing the same God, and thereby opening up possibilities for spiritual and theological inspiration between Christians and Jews.

If Jewish-Christian relations could advance beyond the classical threat of loss of Jewish identity through conversion to another religion, I could well envision a world in which these two religions aid one another, rather than compete with one another. If God's presence can be found in the lives of believers of other religions, along with it can be found also example and inspiration for the Jewish religion. Contact with the spiritual lives of other traditions may prove to be one way — clearly not the only way — for exposing Jewish life to a spiritual heritage that is properly its own, and that has been lost through its meanderings in exile. God's presence is the common quest of Christians and Jews. In looking towards the future, seeking God's presence, Judaism may not only cure its own deficiencies, but also find a healing for the painful history of its relationship with Christianity.

Do Muslims and Christians Believe in the Same God?

Reza Shah-Kazemi

"Some god direct my judgment!"

The Prince of Morocco in
The Merchant of Venice, Act II, Scene VII

This is the supplication made by the prince as he is about to take the test that has been set for winning the fair Portia's hand: to rightly guess which of the three chests contains her portrait. Shakespeare may well have been engaging in a playful irony by having the Muslim prince make this supplication. For he must have known that a central tenet of the Islamic mandate was, precisely, to put an end to polytheism. The prince's supplication, though, helps us to see quite starkly the contrast, or rather incommensurability, between polytheism and monotheism: within the first system of belief, there are many gods from which to choose, while the second asserts that there is but one God from whom to seek help and guidance. We should see in the light of this contrast that it is illogical if not absurd to give anything other than an affirmative answer to the question put to us: "Do Muslims and Christians believe in the same God?" If, instead, we were to ask Christians and Muslims the question: Do you believe in one God — in a unique, ultimate Reality from which all things emerge, to which all things return, and by which all things are governed?, the answer would be: of course! If both parties agree that there is only one God, and not many from which to choose to believe or not believe; and if both parties affirm that they believe in God, then the conclusion follows inescapably: Christians and Muslims do believe in the same — the one-and-only — God. "A false god has no existence in the real world," St. Paul tells us, and goes on to affirm: "there is no God but one" (1 Cor. 8:4). The Qur'ān states the same simple principle in the following verse, one of many that restate the first part of the basic creed of Islam, *lā ilāha illa'Llāh*, *"no divinity but God"*: "*There is no God but the one* God" (5:73; emphasis added). The Qur'ān then makes explicit the logical concomitant of this oneness, as regards fellow believers in this one God, by telling Muslims to say to the Christians and Jews: "Our God *(ilāhunā)* and your God *(ilāhukum)* is one" (29:46). Fellow monotheists, however much they may disagree about other matters, are as one with regard to the One: they all believe in God *as such*, as opposed to believing in such and such a god.

However, once we move from this straightforward monotheistic postulate and enter into theological discussion of the nature of this God in whom all monotheists believe, we encounter major problems. The most insurmountable of these are generated by the Christian doctrines of the Incarnation and the Trinity: Is Jesus God incarnate, and if so, to what extent does this incarnation enter into the definition of the essential nature of God? Is belief in the Trinity an essential condition for authentic belief in God? One kind of Christian position, based on orthodox dogma, can be conceived as follows:

(1) We affirm one God, but this affirmation is articulated in terms of a belief in a Trinity of three Persons: Father, Son, and Spirit.
(2) This belief constitutes an essential element of Christian belief in God.
(3) Anyone who does not share this belief cannot be said to believe in the same God.[1]

Such a position not only answers negatively to the question posed — Muslims and Christians certainly do not believe in the same God — it will also elicit from the Muslim side a correspondingly negative answer: we agree with you, they will say to the Christians, we do not recognize our God, *Allāh*, in the divinity you describe, so we cannot believe in the same God.

---

1. This view, together with a stress on the centrality of the Incarnation to the Christian conception of God, has characterized the response of many leading Evangelicals to the *Common Word* interfaith initiative, an initiative to which reference will be made at the end of this essay.

It would seem that our answer to the question whether Muslims and Christians believe in the same God must therefore comprise both positive and negative elements; it has to be both yes and no: "yes," objectively and metaphysically, and "no," subjectively and theologically. But the objective, metaphysical "yes" outweighs the subjective, theological "no." In other words, Muslims and Christians do indeed believe in the same God, insofar as the ultimate referent of their belief is That to which the word "God" metaphysically refers: the transcendent Absolute, ultimate Reality, the unique source of Being. However, when this same Reality is conceived by human thought, and this conception is framed in theological discourse, with reference to the attributes and acts of this Reality — such as Creator, Revealer, Savior, and Judge — then fundamental differences between the two systems of belief will be apparent. These differences will remain in place for as long as — and insofar as — we remain conceptually bound by the limits of theology; but they can be resolved on the higher plane of metaphysics and the deeper plane of mysticism — planes that are not constrained, doctrinally as regards metaphysics or experientially as regards mysticism, by the limitations of theology.[2]

We will aim to substantiate this argument with reference to two chief sources: the revealed data of the Qur'ān, and the inspired data of the metaphysicians and mystics of both Christianity and Islam. The Qur'ān — and the Sunna or Conduct of the Prophet, which is an eloquent commentary thereon — provides us with compelling evidence that the supreme Object of belief and worship is God for both Muslims and Christians, even if the conceptions of God held by Muslims and Christians diverge and, at points, contradict each other. The perspectives of such mystics as Ibn al-ʿArabī in Islam, and Meister Eckhart in Christianity, help to reveal the manner in which these divergent subjective conceptions of God fail to infringe upon the objective one-and-only-ness of the Absolute believed in by Muslims and Christians. The Absolute referent of the word "God"/"*Allāh*," then, is one and the same when our focus is on the transcendent Object of belief,

---

2. If it be asked what is the difference between theology and metaphysics we would reply as follows, basing ourselves on the writings of René Guénon and Frithjof Schuon: theology is rational thought focused upon the data of revelation, while metaphysics is the rational expression of intellection, intuition, or inspiration, which is proportioned both to the substance of revelation and its source, that is, the Revealer, or the divine reality *per se*. The two are by no means mutually exclusive; indeed, as Palamite "mystical theology," in particular, demonstrates, theology can be enriched by the intellectual insights of metaphysics and by the experiential certitudes of the mystics.

rather than the human subject adhering to the belief: if the word "belief" be defined principally in terms of the divine Object rather than the human subject, then our answer to the question posed must be in the affirmative.

We cannot of course ignore the subjective side of the question, for "belief" implies both things, an object and a subject; but even here, we can answer affirmatively, if the belief of the human subject be defined more in terms of spiritual orientation than mental conception, focusing more on the inner essence of faith than on its outer form. This determination to focus on the essential elements of faith within the subject, rather than the relatively accidental features of conceptual belief, reflects our concern with what is most essential in the divine Object of faith — namely, ultimate Reality — rather than derivative, dogmatically expressed aspects of that Reality. Muslims will not be able to affirm belief in "the Trinity" any more than Christians, on the plane of theology, can unequivocally affirm belief in what Muslims call "*Allāh*"; for this term has come to imply complex theological beliefs articulated in terms of a whole myriad of premises, assumptions, and foundations, the acceptance of all, or most, of which is necessary for the theological affirmation of belief in *Allāh*. If, however, attention is directed away from the theological definition of *Allāh*, and to its supratheological or metaphysical referent — that ultimate Essence *(al-Dhāt)* which is absolutely ineffable and thus unnameable; and if, likewise, we look beyond the theological definition of the Trinitarian conception of God, and focus instead on its supratheological or metaphysical referent — the "superessential One," to quote St. Dionysius, to whom we will turn later — then we shall be in a position to affirm that, despite the different names by which the ultimate Reality is denoted in the two traditions, the Reality thus alluded to is indeed one and the same. And we are justified in referring to this Reality as "God," "Deus," "Theos," or "*Allāh*," or whatever term stands for this Reality in any language, as long as it be made clear that we are not implying thereby all the theological ramifications of these different terms. Rather, we are using these terms to denote their ultimate transcendent referent.

This essay is composed of three parts: the first begins with a discussion of the Qur'ān, and proceeds to address the debates and polemics generated by the Trinitarian conception of God in Christianity. Here it will be seen that the very nature of theological debate renders it all but inevitable that fundamental disagreements about the nature of God will prevail, overshadowing or even undermining the elements of commonality in beliefs held by Muslims and Christians. The second part then shifts to the plane of metaphysics, beginning with discussion of an act of the Prophet, an act of great symbolic significance, which resolves the apparent contradiction between, on the one hand, the Qur'ānic affirmation that the God of the Muslims and the Christians (and the Jews) is one and the same; and, on the other, the Muslim repudiation of the Trinity. The mystics of the two traditions help us to arrive at a position of divine "objectivity," a conceptual point of reference derived from a spiritual perspective *sub specie aeternitatis,* a point of view from which the unique metaphysical Object of belief takes priority over the theologically divergent, subjectively variegated conceptions of that Object. Finally, in part three, we return to the plane of theology in the context of contemporary interfaith dialogue, and evaluate the extent to which the well-intentioned efforts of Muslims and Christians to affirm that we do believe in the same God might benefit from the insights of the mystics, by maintaining a clear distinction between the level of spiritual essence, on which there can be agreement, and that of theological form, on which there is — and should be — respectful disagreement.[3]

1. Qur'ānic Revelation and Muslim-Christian Theological Disputation

The key theological controversy to be addressed here is, quite evidently, that surrounding the Trinitarian conception of God: Does the Christian belief in a Trinitarian God necessarily imply for both Christians and for Muslims that Christians believe in a God quite other than that believed in by Muslims? The Trinity, expressing the belief that God is one and He is three; together with the Incarnation, expressing the belief that God became man, was crucified, and rose from the dead, thereby liberating humanity from sin — these beliefs fly in the face of the central tenets of

3. This is an application of the principle finely articulated by James Cutsinger, "Disagreeing to Agree: A Christian Response to *A Common Word*" (unpublished, but see the online version at www.cutsinger.net/scholarship/articles.shtml). Cutsinger argues that Christians and Muslims can disagree on the level of theology in order to agree on that of metaphysics. This argument is based upon the teachings of Frithjof Schuon, whose perspective on this question is summed up in the formula: conform to holy separation at the base in order to realize holy union at the summit. See Frithjof Schuon, *Logic and Transcendence: A New Translation with Selected Letters,* ed. James S. Cutsinger (Bloomington: World Wisdom, 2009), p. 195.

Muslim faith. The most fundamental aspect of the Muslim creed is centered on an affirmation of divine oneness *(Tawḥīd)*, one of the most important Qur'ānic formulations, and one that explicitly rejects that which lies at the core of Christian belief, the idea that God could have a "son." Chapter 112 of the Qur'ān, titled "Purity" or "Sincerity" *(Sūrat al-Ikhlāṣ)*, reads as follows:

> Say: He, God, is One,
> God, the Eternally Self-Subsistent;
> He begetteth not, nor is He begotten
> And there is none like unto Him.

There is evidently a theological impasse here, a fundamental incompatibility between the respective conceptual forms taken by belief in the same God. Even if Christians retort to the above verses by denying any kind of carnal relation in the "sonship" of Jesus, insisting that the sonship in question does not occur in time and space, but is an eternal principle, of which the historical Incarnation is but an expression,[4] it is nonetheless clear that the Qur'ān emphatically rejects the idea that "sonship" — whether physical, metaphorical, or metaphysical — should form part of any creedal statement regarding God. In other words, it rejects the validity of ascribing to Jesus the status of "son of God," and in so doing rejects a belief that constitutes a cardinal tenet of Christian faith. Likewise, in relation to the Trinity: the Christians are instructed by the Qur'ān to desist from all talk of threeness in relation to God: "Say not 'three'; desist, it would be better for you. God is but one divinity *(innamā Allāh ilāh wāhid)*" (4:171).

One God: Qur'ānic Affirmations

Alongside this critique of certain aspects of Christian belief, the Qur'ān also contains a large number of affirmations, implicit and explicit, that the God worshiped by the Christians (and Jews) is none other than the God

---

4. They also point out that the idea that Jesus "became" the son of God when he was born, or when he was baptized, or at some other point in his life — all such ideas are strictly heretical, being so many forms assumed by the heresy known as "Adoptionism." See Geoffrey Parrinder, *Jesus in the Qur'ān* (London: Sheldon Press, 1965), p. 127.

worshiped by Muslims; the Revealer of the Qur'ān is the Revealer of all the scriptures contained in both the Old and New Testaments; this Revealer is none other than the one God, Creator of the heavens and the earth. It is part of a Muslim's belief that God, as the source of life and love, wisdom and compassion, has revealed messages concerning Himself to *all* human communities, in different ways, and at different times;[5] and that these revelations, from "above," are so many means by which our innate certainty of God from "within" is aroused, awakened, and perfected. This belief is clearly articulated by numerous verses of the Qur'ān. The Muslim is enjoined by the Qur'ān to believe in "God and His Angels, and His Books, and His Prophets" and to affirm: "we do not distinguish between His Messengers" (2:285). More explicitly, the Muslim is instructed: "Say: We believe in God, and that which was revealed unto Abraham, and Ishmael, and Isaac, and Jacob, and the tribes, and that which was given unto Moses and Jesus and the prophets from their Lord. We make no distinction between any of them, and unto Him we have submitted" (2:136). Given the fact that it is the one and only God who has revealed Himself to the Biblical Prophets, to Jesus and to Muhammad, it is this one and only God that, according to the logic of the Qur'ān, is objectively "believed in" by Muslims, Christians, and Jews in the measure of their fidelity to their respective revelations. The Absolute — however it be referred to in different languages, whether proto-Semitic, Hebrew, Syriac, Aramaic, Arabic, or any other language — is That in which belief is invested; it is That which transcends not only the names and concepts by which it is approximately designated, but also the theologies that unfold from it, and by which it becomes enveloped and all too often obscured.[6]

The following verses are of particular relevance to our theme: "He hath ordained for you of the religion that which He commended unto Noah, and that which We reveal to thee [Muhammad], and that which We commended unto Abraham and Moses and Jesus, saying: Establish the re-

---

5. "For every community there is a Messenger" (10:47).

6. Al-Ghazzālī, despite being a master-theologian himself, was essentially a Sufi mystic, and says that theology can be a "veil" over God; only spiritual effort *(mujāhada)* can disclose the true nature of God, His essence and attributes. See his *Iḥyā' 'ulūm al-dīn* (Beirut: Dār al-Jīl, 1992), p. 34; English translation by Nabih Amin Faris, *The Book of Knowledge* (Lahore: Sh. Muhammad Ashraf, 1970), p. 55. Eric Ormsby sums up well al-Ghazzālī's calibrated approach to theology: "It was a weapon, essential for defending the truths of the faith, but not an instrument by which truth itself could be found . . . it demolishes but it does not build." Eric Ormsby, *Ghazali: The Revival of Islam* (Oxford: Oneworld, 2008), p. 64.

ligion, and be not divided therein . . ." (42:13). A single Judeo-Christian-Muslim tradition is here being affirmed, one that is inwardly differentiated, each of the Prophets coming to affirm and renew what was revealed by his predecessor. The key characteristic defining the relationship between the different Prophets is *confirmation:*

> And We caused Jesus, son of Mary, to follow in their footsteps [the footsteps of the Jewish Prophets], confirming that which was [revealed] before him in the Torah, and We bestowed upon him the Gospel wherein is guidance and light, confirming that which was [revealed] before it in the Torah — a guidance and an admonition unto those who are pious. Let the People of the Gospel judge by that which God hath revealed therein. (5:46-47)

The very next verse, 5:48, begins with the following words, reinforcing this crucial role of reciprocal confirmation. "And unto thee [Muhammad] We have revealed the Scripture with the truth, confirming whatever Scripture was before it, and as a guardian over it."

The logical consequence of the assertions of the unique source of revelation for all three traditions is the Qur'ān's categorical affirmation that the God worshiped by the Christians and the Jews ("the People of the Book") is the selfsame God worshiped by Muslims:

> And argue not with the People of the Book except in a manner most fine — but not with those who are oppressors, and say: We believe in that which hath been revealed unto us and that which hath been revealed unto you; our God *(ilāhunā)* and your God *(ilāhukum)* is One, and unto Him we submit. (29:46)

This verse gives us the most definitive answer to the question we have been asked, the *ilāh* or "divinity" believed in by the Muslims and the "People of the Book" — Jews, Christians, and Sabeans — is one and the same. The word *Allāh,* it should be noted, is derived from the word *ilāh* together with the definite article, *al-;* the construct *al-ilāh,* "the divinity," was transformed into the proper name, *Allāh.* This name, therefore, refers intrinsically and metaphysically to "the divinity," to That which is worshiped, to the Absolute. It is also etymologically equivalent to the Hebrew *Elôh,* and the Syriac *Alāh.* All three Semitic forms of this name for the Absolute are in turn derived from the root *'lh,* meaning "to worship."[7] Similarly, in regard to the English word "God," we should note that an identical meaning is conveyed by its etymological root: for it is the past participle construction of the proto-Indo-European root *gheu,* meaning "to invoke/supplicate." The literal meaning of "God" is thus "the One who is invoked (or supplicated)." On this semantic plane, then, we should see no discrepancy between *"Allāh"* and "God" — both are simply semantic forms of designating the divinity to which worship and prayer are directed.[8]

The argument deriving from the above verse can be reinforced by several other verses, among which the following is one of the most important. According to most commentators, this was the first verse revealed granting permission to the Muslims to fight in self-defense against aggressors. It is of particular pertinence to our theme, underlining as it does the duty of Muslims to protect fellow-believers in the Christian and Jewish communities — thus inducing a spirit of solidarity among all those who believe in the one and only God:

> Permission [to fight] is given to those who are being fought, for they have been wronged, and surely God is able to give them victory; those who have been expelled from their homes unjustly, only because they said: Our Lord is God. Had God not driven back some by means of others, monasteries, churches, synagogues and mosques — wherein the name of God is oft-invoked *(yudhkaru fīhā ism Allāh kathīran)* — would assuredly have been destroyed. (22:39-40)

"The name of God" *(ism Allāh)* — the one and only, selfsame God — is "invoked" in monasteries, churches, and synagogues, and not just in mosques. Just as in Islamic theology, the one God has ninety-nine "Names," without thereby becoming anything other than one, so the different "names" given to God in the different revelations do not make the object named anything but one. The names of God revealed by God in these revelations are thus to be seen in stark contrast to those "names" manufactured by the polytheists as labels for their idols. These false gods are described as follows: "They are but names that ye have named, ye and your fathers, for which God hath revealed no authority" (53:23). One is re-

---

7. Umar F. Abd-Allāh, "One God, Many Names," in *Seasons — Semiannual Journal of Zaytuna Institute* 2, no. 1 (2004): 47.

8. Abd-Allāh, "One God, Many Names," p. 51.

minded here of St. Paul's dictum, cited at the outset: "A false god has no existence in the real world."

The various names by which God is named in the Judeo-Christian-Islamic tradition, on the contrary, do have "authority." They refer to one and the same Reality in a manner at once authoritative and authentic, precisely on account of having been revealed by that Reality. These names, therefore, resonate not only with that supreme Reality transcending all thought and language, but also with the innate knowledge of God that articulates the in-most reality of the human soul, the *fitra*.[9] The point here is that it is the same God who creates each soul with innate knowledge of Him, the same God who reveals Himself to all souls in diverse ways, and the same God who is worshiped by the communities defined by these revelations. It is for this rea-son, among others, that the Qur'ān holds out the promise of salvation not just to Muslims but to "Jews, Christians and Sabeans," bringing these three specifically mentioned religious communities into the generic category of believers who combine faith with virtue, these two being the key conditions — necessary but not sufficient[10] — for salvation:

> Truly those who believe [in this Revelation], and the Jews and the Christians and the Sabeans — whoever believeth in God and the Last Day and performeth virtuous deeds — their reward is with their Lord, neither fear nor grief shall befall them. (2:62; repeated almost verbatim at 5:69)

For our purposes, the key part of this verse is the category: "whoever believeth in God." The category is not restricted to just Muslims, Jews, Christians, and Sabeans, but encompasses all those who believe in "God" as such — whatever be the specific name by which God is referred to. This is repeated at the end of the verse: the reward to those who believe and act virtuously is given from "their Lord," *Rabbihim*, whatever be the means by which the Lord as such is designated linguistically.

---

9. This primordial nature is the inalienable infrastructure not just of the soul, but also of the "right religion." There can be no revelation from on high without innate receptiv-ity to that revelation being present within: "So set thy purpose for religion with unswerving devotion — the nature [framed] of God *(fitrat Allāh),* according to which He hath created man. There is no altering God's creation. That is the right religion *(al-dīn al-qayyim),* but most men know not" (30:30).

10. For, according to a well-known saying of the Prophet, nobody is saved on account of his deeds: only the mercy of God affords access to Paradise.

The People of the Book are not told to first ensure that their conception of God corresponds exactly to the Islamic conception, and then to believe in the Last Day, and to act virtuously; rather, it is taken for granted that That which is referred to as *Allāh* is the God in whom they already believe, the God who created them and revealed to them the scriptures by which they are guided. Similarly, in the very same verse in which the Prophet is told not to follow the "whims" *(ahwā')* of the People of the Book, he is also told not only to affirm belief in their scripture, but also to affirm that *Allāh* is "our Lord and your Lord":

And be thou upright as thou art commanded and follow not their whims. Instead say: I believe in whatever scripture God hath revealed, and I am commanded to be just among you. God is our Lord and your Lord. Unto us, our works, and unto you, yours: let there be no argument between us. God will bring us together, and unto Him is the journeying. (42:15)

If, as we shall see below, there is indeed an "argument" between the Muslims and the Christians, over the Trinity, for example, this argument does not pertain to the question of whether Muslims and Christians believe in the same God, or have the same Lord; rather, the argument is over something more contingent: the human conceptualization of that Lord, together with His attributes and acts. *That* He is "our Lord" is not disputed — we all believe in Him; how "our Lord" is conceived by us — that is the subject of the dispute. Unity on the level of the divine Object goes hand in hand with diversity — and even contradiction — on the level of the human subject.

The verses we have cited demonstrate that there is an essential and definitive aspect to faith in "God," which takes precedence over the conceptual and dogmatic forms assumed by that faith. This essential faith is not necessarily annulled by an imperfect conception of That in which one has faith. The positing of two unequal degrees of faith, the one essential and definitive, the other formal and derivative, is principally based on the Qur'ānic verses expressing these two attitudes to the Christian "faith," on the one hand affirmative and on the other critical; it is also derived, as we shall see later, from an act of the Prophet which serves as an implicit commentary, at once dramatic and eloquent, on these two aspects of the Qur'ānic discourse.

The Trinity: Muslim Critique

Before looking at this crucial act of the Prophet, let us consider the critique of the Trinity found in the Qur'ān, and then elaborated in Muslim theology. Although the idea of "threeness" is censured in a general way in the Qur'ān, the only specific "trinity" mentioned in the Qur'ān is not the Trinity affirmed in Christian dogma. On the one hand, both the specific belief in Jesus as the son of God and the general idea of threeness are rejected:

> O People of the Book, do not exaggerate in your religion nor utter about God aught save the truth. The Messiah, Jesus son of Mary, was but a Messenger of God and His Word which He cast into Mary and a Spirit from Him. So believe in God and His Messengers, and say not: "Three"! Desist: it will be better for you. For God is One divinity *(Allāh ilāh wāhid)* — Far removed from His Majesty that He should have a son. . . . (4:171)

On the other hand, a specific configuration of the "trinity"[11] is given in this verse:

> And behold! God will say: "O Jesus, son of Mary! Didst thou say unto men, 'Take me and my mother for two gods beside God?'" He will say: "Glory be to Thee! Never could I say that to which I had no right." (5:116)

This "trinity" is evidently one that all orthodox Christians would similarly reject. As for 4:171, let us look at how it is interpreted by one of the most influential commentators in the specifically theological tradition of exegesis, Fakhr al-Dīn al-Rāzī:

> The first issue: the meaning is, "Do not say that God, glorified be He, is one Substance *(jawhar)* and three hypostases *(aqānīm)*." Know that the doctrine of the Christians is very obscure. What can be gleaned from it is that they affirm one essence *(dhāt)* that is qualified by three attributes *(sifāt)*, except that even though they call them attributes,

---

11. Another form of the "trinity" is given at 5:72: "They indeed disbelieve who say that God is the third of three." This, similarly, refers not to the orthodox Christian Trinity, but to a heretical form thereof.

they are in reality essences *(dhawāt)*. . . . Though they call them "attributes," they are actually affirming the existence of several self-subsisting essences *(dhawāt qā'ima bi-anfusihā)*, and this is pure unbelief *(kufr)*. . . . If, however, we were to understand from these "Three" as meaning that they affirm three attributes, then there can be no denying [the truth of] this. How could we [as Muslims] say otherwise, when we [are the ones who] say, "He is God other than whom there is no god, the King, the Holy, the Peace, the Knower, the Living, the Omnipotent, the Willer etc.," and understand [as we do] each one of these expressions as being distinct from all the others. There can be no other meaning for there being several attributes. Were it unbelief to affirm the existence of several divine attributes, the Qur'ān in its entirety would be refuted; and the intellect would also be invalidated since we necessarily know that the concept[12] of God being Knower *('āliman)* is other than the concept of Him being Omnipotent *(qādiran)* or Living *(hayyan)*.[13]

Even if the "trinity" being refuted here is conceived as consisting of the Father, Jesus, and Mary, the Muslim critique, based on such verses as those cited above, is focused on the Christian idea of three Persons being identical to the one Essence, each Person being absolutely identical to the Essence at the same time as being distinct from the other two Persons. This appears to posit three distinct essences rather than three attributes of one Essence, and thus contrasts sharply with the Muslim theologian's definition of the attributes-Essence relationship. Al-Ghazzālī, for example, gives the standard Sunni-Ash'ari position on the attributes, to which Rāzī also subscribed,[14] as follows: the essential attributes of God — living, knowing, powerful, willing, hearing, seeing, speaking[15] — are "superadded" *(zā'ida)*

12. Literally: "that which is understood from," *mafhūm.*

13. Fakhr al-Dīn al-Rāzī, *Al-Tafsīr al-kabīr* (Beirut: Dar Ehia Al-Tourath Al-Arabi, 2000), vol. 4, pp. 271-72. I am grateful to Dr. Feras Hamza for pointing out to me the importance of this passage.

14. For a helpful introduction to this theme, see Nader al-Bizri, "God's Essence and Attributes," in *The Cambridge Companion to Classical Islamic Theology*, ed. Tim Winter (Cambridge: Cambridge University Press, 2008), especially pp. 129-31.

15. These are the "essential attributes" *(sifāt al-dhāt)* as opposed to attributes of actions *(sifāt al-fi'l)*; the essential attributes are most often deemed to be these seven, but sometimes there are just two (life and knowledge), sometimes eight, at other times fifteen, etc. There was considerable variation as regards what constituted an essential attribute.

to the Essence; these attributes are uncreated and eternal *(qadīma)*, but are not self-subsistent; rather they "subsist through the Essence" *(qā'ima bi'l-dhāt);* they are not identical to the Essence but neither are they other than it.[16] Whereas these Muslim theologians maintain that the attributes subsist not through themselves, but through the Essence, with which they are co-eternal, they understand the Christian view of the Trinity to be, in contrast, a form of *shirk,* "association" or polytheism, insofar as it posits three Persons who are all deemed to be God while also being eternally distinct from each other; each Person being eternally distinguished from the other two while sharing a common substance or nature *(homoousia).* Rāzī says, however, that if the Christians confined themselves to affirming only that God had three attributes, attributes that were clearly subordinate to the Essence they qualify — thus positing a unique Essence that unambiguously transcended the Persons — then they could not be accused of *kufr* or of *shirk.*

The kind of reconciliation of the two theologies being proposed by Rāzī is one whereby the Christians uphold the transcendence of the unique Essence vis-à-vis the three Persons, or affirm the transcendence of the "Father" understood as the Essence, who then manifests Himself through two attributes; this is meant to replace the conception of the Essence, being as it were "shared" equally by the three Persons who are simultaneously identical to the Essence *and* distinguishable as Persons within the Essence. Rāzī would contend that the distinctiveness of the Persons cannot be situated at the same level of absoluteness as the Essence: if the Persons are to be viewed as attributes, then they cannot be distinct from each other on the same plane on which their identity with the Essence is affirmed.

Various efforts were in fact made to narrow the gap between the two theologies along just these lines. These were formulated for the most part by Christian apologists living in Muslim lands, who attempted to do more or less what Rāzī proposed: present the Trinity in terms that resemble the relationship established within Islamic theology between the attributes and the Essence.[17] For example, the Jacobite[18] Christian Arab, Yahyā b.

---

16. *Al-iqtisād fi'l-i'tiqād,* ed. H. Atay and I. Cubkcu (Ankara: Nur Matbaasi, 1962), pp. 4-5.

17. Sidney Griffith effectively refutes Harry Wolfson's claim that the Muslim theologians derived their view of the attributes from the Christian Trinity, showing that it was the other way around: Christians in Muslim lands came to frame their Trinitarian theology in terms already established within Muslim *kalām,* as will be evident in what follows.

18. The Jacobites, Melkites, and Nestorians were the main Christian sects in the territories conquered by the Muslims in the eastern part of the Byzantine empire, principally

'Adī (d. 974), writing in Arabic and making full use of Arabic terms drawn from the vocabulary of Muslim *kalām*, refers to God as being one "substance" *(jawhar)* and three "attributes" *(sifāt)*, each of which is described as being distinct from the other two as regards "meaning" *(ma'nā)*.[19] He was sensitive to the charge of polytheism, and refers to the "ignorant" *(al-juhhāl)* among the Christians who assert that the three hypostases each constitute a distinct substance. The proper conception of the Trinity, according to Yahyā, is based upon the doctrines of the Church Fathers, and it is this conception that is held by "the three sects of the Christians," by which he means the Melkites, the Nestorians, and the Jacobites. The one substance or *ousia* is defined in terms of the Arabic concepts *jawhar* (substance), *dhāt* (essence), and *māhiyya* (quiddity) — all of which were applied by Muslim theologians to God. Within this unique substance, however, one can distinguish between three Persons who are defined by unique "personal" properties: paternity *(ubūwa)* for the Father, filiation *(bunūwa)* for the Son, and procession *(inbi'āth)* for the Spirit.[20]

In the previous century, another Arab Christian, the Nestorian Ammār al-Basrī (d. ca. 850), had rebutted the charge of tri-theism leveled against the Christians by the Muslims, and articulated in his *Kitāb al-Burhān* ("The Book of Proof") a position very close to that proposed by Rāzī:

> Before God, we are blameless of alleging three gods. Rather, by our saying Father, Son and Holy Spirit, we want no more than to substantiate the statement that God is living *(hayy)*, speaking *(nātiq)*. And the Father is the one whom we consider to have life *(hayāt)* and word *(kalima)*. The life is the Holy Spirit and the word is the Son.[21]

Syria, Mesopotamia, and Persia, in the first wave of the expansion of Islam. They were distinguished principally by different Christologies. As Sidney Griffith shows clearly, these Christian sects were not only granted tolerance by the Muslims, their identity was in large part forged by the culture of Islam, which "fostered the articulation of a new cultural expression of Christian doctrine, this time in Arabic, and it provided the cultural framework within which the several Christian denominations of the Orient ultimately came to define their mature ecclesial identities." Sidney Griffith, *The Church in the Shadow of the Mosque: Christians and Muslims in the World of Islam* (Princeton and Oxford: Princeton University Press, 2008), p. 4.

19. See Sidney Griffith, *The Beginnings of Christian Theology in Arabic: Muslim-Christian Encounters in the Early Islamic Period* (Aldershot, UK: Ashgate, 2002), p. 177.

20. See Harry A. Wolfson, *The Philosophy of the Kalam* (Cambridge, MA: Harvard University Press, 1976), pp. 335-36.

21. Cited in Griffith, *Beginnings*, p. 170.

This presentation echoes that of St. Irenaeus, one of the earliest Church Fathers (d. ca. 202), who referred to the Son and the Spirit as being akin to the "two hands" of God the Father, by which He creates all things, such that the Father comes to creation through the Son and in the Spirit, and creatures go to the Father in the Spirit and through the Son. St. Irenaeus refers to the Son as the Word of God, and the Spirit as the Wisdom of God; these two were eternally present in God and with God, without dividing Him into three: "since to Him is ever present His Word and Wisdom, the Son and the Spirit, by whom and in whom He made all things."[22]

Here, the derivative aspect of the divinity of the second and third Persons of the Trinity, in relation to the first, is combined with the unity of the Godhead — the two "hands" being inseparable from the "body" of the person to whom they belong. To the objection that God is not composed of parts, and cannot be compared to a body with two hands, St. Irenaeus would no doubt respond by saying that one has to apply to this analogy a strong *mutatis mutandis* clause: God's "body" — the divine Reality — is absolute simplicity, thus noncomposite; His "hands" — that is, His Word and His Wisdom — are akin to the hands of a body only in one respect. Just as it is through the hands that the body acts, so it is through the divine Word and Wisdom that God creates. In another respect, however, there is no common measure between the two things compared, for the Word and Wisdom are inseparable from the very simplicity of God's Reality, whereas the two hands of a body can be separated from the body of which they are relatively accidental parts, both the body and its hands being composite substances.

Another Christian Arab, the Jacobite Abū Rā'ita (d. ca. 850) pursued a similar line of thought to that of 'Ammār al-Basrī, making use of the Muslim attributes of knowledge and life. Just as Muslim theologians accept that God is "the Knowing" *(al-'Alīm)* and "the Living" *(al-Hayy)*, without these attributes being considered as "partners" *(shurakā', singular sharīk)* alongside God, so, for the Christians, these two attributes are given the names "Son" and "Spirit": "Furthermore, as perfect entities, God's life and knowledge must be considered not only as distinguishable, but also as simultaneously in union *(ittisāl)* with one another, and with His perfect being."[23] God's life and knowledge are thus hypostases *(aqānīm)*,[24] which are

---

22. St. Irenaeus, *Five Books of S. Irenaeus Against Heresies,* trans. John Keble (Oxford and London: James Parker & Co., 1872), Book 4, ch. 20.1, pp. 364-65.

23. Griffith, *Beginnings,* p. 183.

24. This is the plural of *uqnūm,* the Arabic transliteration of the Syriac *qnoma,* which translates the Greek *hypostasis.* Griffith, *Beginnings,* p. 180.

distinguished one from the other without this distinction rupturing the unity of the substance of God's being.

While such formulations may appear to bridge the gap between the two theologies in some respects, the rapprochement on this level is a fragile one. For the very insistence of the Christian apologists upon the eternal distinction between the Persons of the Trinity at the level of the Godhead, alongside the affirmation that each of the Persons is identical to that Godhead, ensured that most Muslim theologians would not accept the doctrine. Typical of the kind of argument made against the Christian Trinity is that of the philosopher al-Kindī (d. 873). He argued that if, on the one hand, there is a sole substance within each of the hypostases, and on the other, each of the hypostases has a property, which is eternal in it, and which differentiates one hypostasis from the other, it follows that:

> . . . each of the hypostases is composed of a substance, which is common to all of them, and a property, which is unique to each of them. But everything composed is the effect of a cause, and effect of a cause cannot be eternal, whence it follows that neither is the Father eternal nor is the Son eternal nor is the Holy Spirit eternal. Thus, things which have been assumed to be eternal are not eternal.[25]

Yahyā b. ʿAdī cites Kindī's critique and retorts: this argument holds only for created substances; the composite nature of created things is a concomitant of their temporality, cause and effect only taking place in time. In the case of the Persons of the Trinity, however, the temporal condition is transcended: they have never not existed, thus they cannot have been brought into a composite form comprising substance and property. On the contrary, "the substance is described by every one of these attributes *(al-sifāt)* and . . . these attributes are eternal, without their having been produced in it after they had not been."[26]

Kindī would probably have responded that the composite nature of a compound is not contingent upon temporality alone; rather, it is a property of the substance of the thing itself: any substance composed of more than one element cannot but be regarded as composite, it cannot be simple. It is the fact of the existence of two or more elements that makes a sub-

25. Cited in Wolfson, *Philosophy of the Kalam*, p. 322.
26. Cited in Wolfson, *Philosophy of the Kalam*, p. 322.

stance compound; the question of time does not enter into the essential definition of substance.

In any case, Yaḥyā b. ʿAdī is trying here to answer Muslim objections to the Trinity, while bringing the focus back to something he thinks is common between the Muslim and Christian conceptions of unity and plurality in relation to God. He argues that, like the Muslim attributes, the Christian Trinity is an eternally subsistent mode of plurality within unity; it is a threeness pertaining to the unique substance of divinity, with the real distinctiveness of each Person being maintained within that one substance. But the problems remain, as is well demonstrated by the following polemical exchange — among the most protracted in all such exchanges that have been recorded in the history of Muslim-Christian polemics. The correspondence began with a letter written in the thirteenth century by Paul of Antioch, the Melkite Bishop of Sidon, to "a Muslim friend." This apology for the Christian faith went through various editions, one of which was sent by "the people of Cyprus" to two Muslim theologians in Damascus, Ibn Taymiyya in 1316 and Ibn Abī Ṭālib al-Dimashqī in the following year. As regards the Trinity, the letter echoes the argument of ʿAmmār al-Basrī, noted above. It asserts: "The three names [Father, Son, and Spirit] are one eternal and everlasting God: a thing living and articulate *(shayʾ ḥayy nāṭiq)*, the Essence, speech, life. As we see it, the Essence is the Father, the speech is the Son, and the life is the Holy Spirit." The response from al-Dimashqī concentrates on the distinction between the named entities, arguing that each named being is utterly different from the other two, "the Father is different from the Son, and utterly distinct from him, and similarly the Spirit is different from both of them." Given the affirmation of these three apparently discrete entities, the result can only be *kufr* (unbelief) and *shirk* (polytheism).

> In this way you declare unbelief and polytheism by declaring that the Father exists by his essence, that is, he is eternal, and that he is living by the Spirit, and articulating by the Son; that the Spirit is living by its essence, that is, it is eternal, and that it exists by the Father, and is articulating by the Son; and that the Son is articulating by his essence, that is, he is eternal, and he exists by the Father and is living by the Spirit. Thus you give the clearest indication of polytheism.[27]

27. Cited in Rifaat Ebied and David Thomas, eds., *Muslim-Christian Polemic during the Crusades: The Letter from the People of Cyprus and Ibn Abi Ṭālib's Response* (Leiden: Brill, 2005), p. 333 (translation modified).

In other words, we return to the objection made by Rāzī: the Persons are not attributes *(sifāt)*, but are in reality essences *(dhawāt)*, each essence being defined by a property particular to it: existence is the eternally subsistent defining property — hence the eternal "essence" — of the Father; life is the eternally subsistent defining property — hence the eternal "essence" — of the Spirit; and articulation is the eternally subsistent defining property — hence the eternal "essence" — of the Son. We should make it clear here that Dimashqī's response is based on the classical Ashʿarite formula, mentioned above by al-Ghazzālī: the attributes must be described as being neither God nor other than God. This ambivalent formula, alone, is deemed to satisfy the requirement of simultaneously safeguarding the divine unity while affirming the reality of the attributes in their distinctiveness. Let us look at this formula more closely:

(1) "not God": The attributes are truly distinct in their plurality, but they cannot be said to constitute different essences alongside God, and this is why, in their distinctive plurality, they must not be identified purely and simply with the Absolute: the attributes, in this respect, are thus "other than God." And this is what the Christian formulations of the Essence-Person (or Essence-attribute) relationship fail to assert; they maintain, on the contrary, that each Person of the Trinity — even if this Person be described as a Muslim-sounding "attribute" — is identified with God, at the same time as having its own distinctiveness as a Person.

(2) "not other than God": The Ashʿarites add to the preceding denial the complementary affirmation that the attributes are "not other than God," for the attributes have no self-subsistent essences of their own, and subsist only through the unique divine Essence. But this affirmation "not other than God" can only be accepted if it be conditioned by the negation: the attributes are "not God." The resulting synthesis of the two complementary statements affirms the reality of the attributes without undermining the unity of God, while upholding the unity of God without denying the reality of the attributes. For the Ashʿarites, then, all the attributes are co-eternal with the Essence, not being absolutely "other" than It, nor being absolutely identified with It; thus they are *real* and not simply metaphors or mere names, but their reality does not introduce division within the one Essence.

At this point one should note that it is not just the Christians who fall short of the Ashʿarite criteria of *tawhīd* on this issue, for both the "attributionists" or "assimilationists" (*al-mushabbiha,* literally: those who create a likeness or similarity), referred to as al-Hashwiyya, and the "antiattributionists," the Muʿtazilites, are regarded as holding erroneous and even heretical beliefs about God. The first group, basing themselves on a literal reading of certain Qurʾānic verses, ascribed to God quasi-corporeal attributes (a body, hands, a face, and so on), thus falling foul of assimilationism *(tashbīh),* or making God comparable to creatures, and anthropomorphism *(tajsīm),* leading to the "sin" of association or polytheism *(shirk);* while their opponents, the Muʿtazilites, are deemed to stray too far in the opposite direction, stripping God *(taʿtīl)* of all attributes in a vain effort to safeguard His transcendent unicity. For them, God can be described as "knowing," but not through an attribute called "knowledge"; He is indeed omnipotent, but not through an attribute called "power."[28] It is pertinent to note here that the accusation of being a "Christian" is made in the disputes over the attributes: the Ashʿarite theologian al-Shahrastānī accuses the Muʿtazilite, Abū al-Hudhayl al-ʿAllāf (d. 841) of imitating the Christians in their view of the relationship between the Essence and the Persons, saying, "ʿAbū Hudhayl's affirmation of these attributes as aspects of the Essence is the same as the hypostases of the Christians."[29]

The Muʿtazilite position is typically based on this kind of reasoning:

1. That which is eternal is divine.
2. The divinity is absolute unity, utter simplicity.
3. The unity and simplicity of God thus strictly excludes the plurality of eternal attributes.

God cannot therefore have attributes that are both eternal and multiple: to assert the contrary is to fall into polytheism.[30] In his argument against those "philosophers" who deny that eternal attributes can be ascribed to God, al-Ghazzālī writes: "Why should it be impossible to say that, just as the essence of Him who is necessary of existence [*wājib al-wujūd,* 'the necessary existent'] is eternal and has no efficient cause, so also His attribute exists with Him from eternity and thus has no efficient cause?" As Wolfson notes, this argument is not so dissimilar from the Christian defense of the Trinity[31] — as we saw above, in Yahyā b. ʿAdī's response to Kindī.

28. Cited by Ignaz Goldziher, *Introduction to Islamic Theology and Law,* trans. A. Hamori and R. Hamori (Princeton: Princeton University Press, 1981), p. 95.

29. Cited in Griffith, *Beginnings,* p. 178.

30. See Wolfson, *Philosophy of the Kalam,* pp. 132-43.

31. Wolfson, *Philosophy of the Kalam,* pp. 139 and 323. As regards Wolfson's claim that

It is thus not surprising to find the Spanish scholar of the Zāhirī school of thought, Ibn al-Hazm (d. 1064), sarcastically asking an Ash'arite: "Since you say that coexistent with God are fifteen attributes, all of them other than He and all of them eternal, why do you find fault with the Christians when they say that God is the 'third of three'?"[32] The Ash'arite, according to Ibn Hazm, lamely replies that the only mistake made by the Christians is restricting to two the number of things coexisting with God. In like fashion, the contemporary Iranian Shi'ite scholar, Ayatollah Javādi-Āmulī, takes the Ash'arites to task for believing in seven, eight, or nine "gods" rather than just the three of the Christians. It is the Ash'arite affirmation of the attributes as being both eternal, on the one hand, and "superadded" to the Essence *(zā'ida 'alā'l-dhāt)*, on the other, that leads Javādi-Āmulī to accuse the Ash'arites of believing in more than one God: "If we accept that there are eight attributes of the Essence, in addition to the Essence itself, then we will have nine eternal existent entities."[33] He mounts a strong argument in favor of the Shi'ite position, which is neither that of simply stripping God's Essence of all attributes *(ta'tīl)*, as did the Mu'tazilites, nor affirming them as being superadded to the Essence, as did the Ash'arites. Rather, for the Shi'is, all of the attributes are viewed as being real, on the one hand, this reality being absolutely identical with the Essence; and, on the other hand, each of the attributes are distinct from the Essence, and thus from each other, only in respect of conceptual meaning *(mafhūm)*.[34]

Furthermore, the strict traditionalists — among them, Hanbalite literalists — pour scorn on *all* those who engage in theology *(kalām)*, saying

---

"Muslims [were led] to adopt a Christian doctrine which is explicitly rejected in the Koran, and transform it into a Muslim doctrine . . . [they were] led to the substitution in Muslim theology of divine attributes for the Christian Trinity" (p. 128), it is clear that the differences between the two doctrines greatly outweigh their similarities.

32. Wolfson, *Philosophy of the Kalam*, p. 314.

33. 'Abd Allāh Javādi-Āmulī, *Tawhīd dar Qur'ān* [Tawhīd in the Qur'ān], vol. 2 of *Tafsīr-i mawdū'ī-i Qur'ān-i Karīm* (Qum: Isrā' Research Centre, 1386 Sh./1998), p. 301.

34. Javādi-Āmulī, *Tawhīd*, pp. 305-11. This perspective is based on such texts as the sermon no. 1 of the *Nahj al-balāgha* of Imam 'Alī b. Abī Tālib. See our translation of and comment upon this seminal text, *Justice and Remembrance: Introducing the Spirituality of Imam 'Alī* (London: I. B. Tauris, 2005), Appendix 1, pp. 208-18. On the one hand, one's conception of the Essence must be shorn of all attributes, insofar as these latter are susceptible to distinctive conception apart from the Essence, and on the other hand, the ontological reality of the attributes is affirmed, each attribute having no "binding limitation," insofar as its substance is identified absolutely with the divine Essence.

that the literal meaning of the Qur'ān and the prophetic Sunna suffice; the use of reason, argument, and disputation only leads astray. The great jurist al-Shāfi'ī, founder of one of the four schools of Sunni jurisprudence, said: "My verdict on the people of *kalām* is that they should be beaten with whips and the soles of sandals, and then paraded through all tribes and encampments, while it is proclaimed of them, 'Such is the reward of those who forsake the Qur'ān and the Sunna, and give themselves up to the *kalām*.'"[35]

It would appear necessary, in the light of these intra-Muslim polemics, to ask the question: Do all Muslims in fact believe in the same God?[36] The same can be said of the Christians, whose mutual anathematizations and excommunications are too many and complex to begin to mention here. Suffice to say that, on the theological plane we are presently considering, we certainly need to ask the question whether and to what extent Catholics and Orthodox believe in the same God, if these two great branches of the church could split so definitively and acrimoniously over the correct understanding of the Trinity: Does the Spirit proceed from the Father alone, as the Orthodox maintain, or from the Father and the Son *(filioque)*, as the Catholics maintain? If this question, going to the very heart of the Trinitarian conception of God, is disputed, then, in the measure that one's belief in God is predicated upon a proper understanding of the Trinity, it is not irrelevant or irreverent to ask the question: Do Catho-

35. Cited by Ignaz Goldziher, *Introduction to Islamic Theology and Law*, pp. 110-11.

36. As we shall see in the next section, Ibn al-'Arabī's metaphysics allows us to answer in the affirmative: yes, Muslims do believe in the same God, as regards the divine essence of belief, even if the human form assumed by belief contradicts other such forms. It might also be noted here that he offers a strictly metaphysical view of the divine attributes, arguing that they are certainly real, but only as the Essence (this being identical to the Shi'i position); but as regards their diversity, he argues that this is not only due to the diverse modes of perfection indistinguishably comprised within the Essence; the diversity is a concomitant also of the plurality of created being, with which the one Essence enters into so many relationships; the attributes are thus so many modes of relationship with the cosmos, and they become outwardly diversified according to the multiplicity of the cosmos. The metaphysical "oneness of being," and not just the oneness of God, is established by Ibn al-'Arabī through his assertion that the multiplicity of the cosmos is rooted in the "fixed archetypes" *(al-a'yān al-thābita)*, and these, in turn, have *no real existence* — no ontological substance. They "exist" only in the consciousness of God, in a manner analogous to the subsistence of ideas within the mind of man. He thus can assert that there is nothing in being but God, and since God is one, being cannot but be one. See William C. Chittick, *The Sufi Path of Knowledge: Ibn al-'Arabī's Metaphysics of Imagination* (Albany: State University of New York Press, 1989), pp. 31-58, et passim.

lics and Orthodox believe in the same God? The question is by no means merely academic, nor of merely historical interest, pertaining only to the "great schism" that was formalized in 1054. As recently as 1848, when Pope Pius IX issued an invitation to the Eastern churches on the subject of unity (in the apostolic letter *In Suprema Petri Apostoli Sede*), he met with a blistering response from the Eastern Patriarchs: how could they unite with the Catholics who professed the *filioque*, "condemned by many Holy Councils . . . subjected to anathema by the eighth Ecumenical Council"; the *filioque*, which introduced unequal relations in the Trinity and, most seriously of all, "destroyed the oneness from the one cause," i.e., the Father:

> The novel doctrine of the Holy Ghost proceeding from the Father and the Son is essentially heresy, and its maintainers, whoever they be, are heretics, according to the sentence of Pope St. Damasus ("If anyone rightly holds concerning the Father and the Son, yet holds not rightly of the Holy Ghost, he is a heretic"), and the congregations of such are also heretical, and all spiritual communion in worship of the orthodox sons of the Catholic Church with such is unlawful.[37]

It is the Catholic addition of the *filioque* that, so the Orthodox argue to this day, undermined the "monarchy" of the Father as sole cause of the Godhead, and thereby ruined the balance between the unity of God — determined by the Father — and the threeness of God established by the Persons. If the Spirit "proceeded" not from the Father alone, but also from the Son, then there are two sources or causes of the Godhead, instead of one. This is what is implied in the accusation that the very oneness of the cause of the Godhead, the Father, is "destroyed" by the addition of the word *filioque* to the Creed.[38]

Can one say, then, that the Orthodox conception of the Trinity, with its sole source of unity located in the Father, is more likely to meet Muslim theological criteria of *Tawhīd*? Not necessarily. For the Trinity remains central to Orthodox theology, and any effort to elevate the unity of God above the Trinity is fraught with problems. Even if the Father is described

37. A. Edward Siecienski, *The Filioque: History of a Doctrinal Controversy* (Oxford: Oxford University Press, 2010), pp. 188-89.

38. See Timothy Ware, *The Orthodox Church* (Harmondsworth, UK: Penguin, 1972 [reprint]), pp. 218-23, for a concise explanation of the doctrinal implications of the *filioque;* and for a more extended theological exposition, Vladimir Lossky, *The Mystical Theology of the Eastern Church* (Cambridge: James Clarke, 2005 [reprint]), pp. 51-66, et passim.

as the uncaused cause of the Son and the Spirit, one cannot call the Father "superior" to them, for any kind of elevation of the Father implies a subordination of the other two Persons. Orthodox theologians firmly resisted any such "subordinationism," as is clear from the following statement by St. Gregory of Nazianzen:

> I should like to call the Father the greater, because from Him flow both the equality and the being of the equals [i.e., the other two Persons]. . . . But I am afraid to use the word Origin, lest I should make Him the Origin of inferiors, and thus insult Him by precedencies of honour. *For the lowering of those who are from Him is no glory to the Source.* . . . Godhead neither increased nor diminished by superiorities or inferiorities; in every respect equal, in every respect the same, just as the beauty and the greatness of the heavens is one; the infinite connaturality of Three Infinite Ones, each God when considered in Himself; as the Father, so the Son, as the Son so the Holy Ghost; the Three, one God, when contemplated together; each God because consubstantial; the Three, one God because of the monarchy.[39]

For the Muslim theologian the principle of unity — "one God because of the monarchy" — is fatally compromised by the assertion of trinity: "each God because consubstantial." The logical consequence of this consubstantiality is that all attributes of the Godhead pertain to each of the three Persons of the Trinity in a quasi-absolute manner: each Person is fully God by dint of sharing the same substance *(homoousia)* of Godhead; they are of the same nature, while being distinct from the others only on account of a particular "personal" quality: "begetting" in the case of the Father, "being begotten" in the case of the Son, and "proceeding from" in the case of the Spirit, as we have seen above. In the words of St. John of Damascus:

> For in their hypostatic or personal properties alone — the properties of being unbegotten, of filiation, and of procession — do the three divine hypostases differ from each other, being indivisibly divided, not by essence but by the distinguishing mark of their proper and peculiar

---

39. Lossky, *The Mystical Theology,* p. 63. To introduce any kind of inequality within the Godhead is to fall into a kind of Arianism, against which St. Gregory of Nazianzen railed: "We believe that to subordinate anything of the Three is to destroy the whole" (from his attack on Arius in the treatise "On St. Basil").

hypostasis. . . . The Father, the Son, and the Holy Ghost are one in all respects save those of being unbegotten, of filiation and of procession.[40]

This statement helps us to perceive the reason why, on the theological plane, it is so difficult to formulate the Trinity in terms that fit within the frame of an Islamic conception of attributes. For according to the dogma of the Trinity — whether Orthodox or Catholic[41] — everything possessed by the Father is equally possessed by the Son and the Spirit; in other words, all the divine attributes such as knowledge, power, will, etc. are ascribed equally to all three Persons, who are distinguished one from the other *exclusively* according to their Personal properties. This view diverges radically from the Islamic conception of the attributes, all of which are possessed by one sole Essence, and each of which is distinguished from all the others by virtue of its particular property or quality; the attribute of knowledge, for example, cannot be equated with that of power, except by virtue of their common root and source in the Essence. According to the Trinity, however, both attributes are equally predicated of each of the three Persons, who are distinguished from each other, not as one attribute is distinct from another, but solely by a personal property defined in relation to origin: "the properties of being unbegotten, of filiation, and of procession," as St. John put it, describing, respectively, the Father, Son, and Spirit.

According to this strict application of the dogma, it is difficult to see how the three Persons constitute different attributes of God, if "attributes" be defined according to Muslim theology. For each of the Persons equally possesses all of the attributes of the other two, with the sole exception of the quality determined by their respective "personal" properties. Apart from this sole distinction, each Person of the Trinity is deemed to be equal to the others insofar as all the divine attributes are concerned; so the Son and the Spirit are as omniscient and omnipotent as the Father, and the same applies to all the attributes. St. Thomas Aquinas, for example, after defining the Son as the Word or the "understanding" of God, writes that in God "*to be* and *to understand* are identical. Therefore, the divine Word that

40. Cited in Lossky, *The Mystical Theology,* p. 54.

41. St. Augustine, for example, in his treatise on the Trinity, maintains that "there is so great an equality in that Trinity that . . . the Father is not greater than the Son in respect to divinity." Cited by Harry A. Wolfson, *The Philosophy of the Church Fathers,* vol. 1: *Faith, Trinity and Incarnation* (Cambridge, MA: Harvard University Press, 1970), p. 357. The Father, the Son and the Spirit are *equally* "divine"; so every attribute of divinity is to be equally attributed to all three Persons.

is in God, whose Word He is according to intellectual existence, has the same existence as God, whose Word He is. Consequently, the Word must be of the same essence and nature as God Himself, and all attributes whatsoever that are predicated of God, must pertain also to the Word of God."[42] The same logic is applied to the Spirit, identified by Aquinas as the love of God for Himself.[43] Thus it is to all three Persons equally that all the attributes of divinity pertain, for each is nothing other than the one substance. It is precisely this "sharing" of all divine attributes that is deemed by Muslim theologians to be a violation of *Tawhīd*, for it appears to posit three differentiated realities that are at once fully divine and yet eternally distinct from each other. It is this that makes theologians like Rāzī claim that, even if the Christians call the three Persons "attributes" of one Essence, they in fact believe in three distinct essences.

The Christian might respond as follows: when it is asserted that the Son or Word possesses all the attributes of the Father, or the Essence, what is meant is that insofar as the divine nature is simple, on the one hand, and insofar as the Son is identified with this nature, on the other, the Son must possess all the attributes possessed by the Father. The Son does not possess all these attributes by virtue of that which defines him as "Son" — his being begotten — but by virtue of his substance, which is identical to that of the Essence. The argument might be extended thus: you Muslims must regard each of the essential divine attributes as equally possessing all the other attributes — failing which the simplicity of the divine nature is violated. Each attribute must possess all the other attributes, not in respect of what distinguishes it as a specific attribute — wisdom, for example, as opposed to power; rather, it can only possess all the other attributes insofar as it is not other than the object of attribution, thus, insofar as it is the one Essence, to which all the essential attributes are ascribed. From this point of view, the Christian might conclude, Muslim belief in a plurality of essential attributes is not so different from the Trinitarian conception of God.

The Ash'arite might reply as follows, beginning with a reminder of the definitive formula: "The attributes are not God and not other than God"; what is missing from the Trinitarian conception is precisely the apophatic element of the formula. The Christian only says that each Per-

---

42. *Aquinas's Shorter Summa: Saint Thomas's Own Concise Version of His Summa Theologica*, trans. Cyril Vollert (Manchester, NH: Sophia Institute, 2002), ch. 41, p. 38.

43. See *Aquinas's Shorter Summa*, chs. 45-48. At the end of this essay we shall see the way in which Aquinas helps to build a bridge between the two theologies — a bridge constructed out of a philosophical conception of the absolute simplicity of the divine Essence.

son is not the other two, but as regards the divine identity of each Person, there is only affirmation and no negation. That is, the Christian only affirms the divinity of all three Persons, without making the negation that would register the relativity of the "Persons" in relation to the pure absoluteness and untrammeled unicity of the Essence. The negation — "not God" — is required as the premise upon which the complementary affirmation — "not other than God" — is valid. The Shi'i theologian would also reject the Trinitarian conception, but for a different reason: the essential attributes are indeed nothing but the Essence, and are thus all equally "God," given the divine simplicity; but what is missing from the Trinitarian conception, from this point of view, is the correct definition of what distinguishes the attributes from each other: they are distinguished not by personal properties of begetting, being begotten, and proceeding, as the Christians would say; rather, they are distinguished only as regards their meaning, that meaning which is conceivable from the human point of view.[44] That which distinguishes one attribute from another is therefore eminently contingent. The Trinitarian, by contrast, not only conceives of the distinctions within the Godhead as being defined according to personal properties, but also conceives of these distinctions as being eternal: the distinctions by which the three Persons are distinguished are eternal distinctions. For both Shi'is and Sunnis, the Persons of the Trinity cannot be at once eternally distinct *and* equally divine. For all Muslim theologians, distinction implies relativity, while divinity implies absolute unity.

All such theological disagreement notwithstanding, the argument made earlier, based on Qur'ānic verses, that the Christians do indeed believe in and worship the selfsame God as the Muslims, is not necessarily invalidated. The question here, for the Muslims, is this: Which aspect takes priority within the Qur'ānic discourse, rejection of Christian dogma or affirmation of Christian belief in the one God? Both aspects, of course, have to be accepted by the Muslim who wishes to be faithful to the Qur'ān, but the challenge is to determine which is to be given priority in the process of synthesizing the two aspects into one fundamental, definitive attitude to Christian belief. We would argue that the aspect of affirmation must take

44. This does not mean that the attributes are merely figments of human imagination, devoid of objective ontological substance; it means, on the contrary, that the one Essence constitutes the ontological reality of the attributes, and that what the human intellect conceives as distinct attributes is but a reflection of the infinite perfections of the Essence, perfections that cannot in any way be distinguished from the absolute infinitude of the Essence, that is: an absolute oneness which is infinitely perfect.

priority, insofar as the *objective* grounds upon which one can affirm that Christians and Muslims believe in the same God prevail over the *subjective* differences of conception of that God. The different conceptions have become embodied in theological dogmas, but we (Muslims) need to ask the question: Do these dogmas define the essence of Christian belief in God? Or is it the case, rather, that the essence of Christian belief in God transcends the dogmas that attempt to define both God and orthodox belief in God? We also need to bring into the argument the crucial principle of intention: insofar as we regard the principle of spiritual intention, governed by the divine Object, as taking precedence over the rational conception, fashioned by the human subject, we can assert that what unites Muslims and Christians — belief in one God and not several gods — is infinitely more significant than what divides them, namely, their respective conceptions of the precise nature, the attributes, and the actions of that God. The Qur'ānic assertion that the God of the Christians and Muslims is one and the same is an assertion relating more to objective reality and to ultimate principle than to subjective perceptions and dogmatic definitions: however the Christians subjectively define their God, the object of their definitions and the ultimate goal of their devotion is the one and only God. This kind of reasoning can help Muslims to arrive at the conclusion that the oneness of the divinity in whom the Christians affirm belief takes priority over the fact that their description of this God entails a Trinity within the Unity. However, in the measure that one's reasoning follows a theological train of thought, the tendency will be in the opposite direction so that, for most Muslim theologians, Trinitarian dogma will be regarded as overshadowing if not eclipsing the unity of God.

2. Beyond Theology

The argument being proposed here might benefit from insights derived from a different approach to the issue, symbolic and metaphysical rather than ratiocinative and theological. An appeal has to be made to spiritual intuition. There is an incident that took place in the life of the Prophet which calls out to be deciphered by precisely this kind of spiritual intuition. It demonstrates graphically that Christians believe in and worship nothing but the one true God. It also shows the importance of affirming solidarity with "fellow-believers," and how this spiritual solidarity must ultimately prevail over all theological differences between them.

In the ninth year after the Hijra (631)[45] a Christian delegation from Najran (in Yemen) came to Medina to engage in theological discussion and political negotiation. For our purposes, the most significant aspect of this event is the fact that when the Christians requested to leave the city to perform their liturgy, the Prophet invited them to accomplish their rites in his own mosque. According to the historian Ibn Isḥāq, who gives the standard account of this remarkable event, the Christians in question were "Malikī" that is, Melkite, meaning that they followed the Byzantine Christian rites. These rites embodied all the fundamental dogmas of the Church Councils, so we are speaking here about an enactment of the very doctrines — Trinity, Sonship, Incarnation — that are criticized in the Qur'ān. Though we do not know exactly what form of liturgy was enacted in the Prophet's mosque, what is known is that Christians were permitted to perform their prayers in the most sacred spot in the Prophet's city — an act that would be unthinkable were these Christians praying to something other than *Allāh*.

Clearly, in this "existential" commentary on the Qur'ānic discourse relating to the Christian faith, it is the supratheological or metaphysical perspective of identity or unity that takes priority over theological divergence. The reality of this divergence is not denied by the prophetic act;[46] rather, the invalidity of drawing certain conclusions from this divergence is revealed: one cannot use the divergence as grounds for asserting that Christians believe in and worship something other than God. The act of the Prophet shows, on the contrary, that disagreement on the plane of dogma can — and should — coexist with spiritual affirmation on the superior plane of ultimate Reality, that Reality of which dogma is an inescapably limited, conceptual expression. Exoteric or theological distinction remains on its own level, and this distinction is necessary for upholding the uniqueness and integrity of each path: ". . . for each of you [communities] We have established *a* Law and *a* Path (5:48; emphasis added)." While metaphysical identity is implied by spiritual intention: the

45. There is some discrepancy in the sources about the precise date of this event. See A. Guillaume, trans., *The Life of Muhammad: A Translation of Ibn Ishaq's Sirat Rasul Allah* (Oxford: Oxford University Press, 1968), pp. 270-77; see also Martin Lings, *Muhammad: His Life Based on the Earliest Sources* (Cambridge: Cambridge University Press, 1984), pp. 324-25.

46. Indeed, the dispute over the nature of Jesus was cut short by a revelation to the Prophet instructing him to challenge the Christians to a mutual imprecation *(mubāhala)*: the curse of God was to be invoked on "those who lie"; see Q 3:61. The challenge was in fact not taken up by the Christians.

summit is One, and the believer moves towards that oneness precisely by obeying the revealed Law and traversing the spiritual Path that leads to that summit: "Unto your Lord is your return, all of you, and He will inform you about those things concerning which ye differed" (5:48, end of the verse).

The Prophet's action thus reinforces the primary thrust of the Qur'ānic message regarding the God of the Christians: it is the same God that is worshiped, but that divinity is conceived differently — erroneously, as each would say about the other. The oneness of the divine Object takes precedence — infinitely, one might add — over any diversity wrought by the human subjects; for that which is spiritually intended by sincere faith takes priority over the verbal and conceptual forms assumed by the intention: these forms are accidental, while the object intended is essential. This spiritual intention manifests an intrinsic "tendency" towards the Transcendent, and this harmonizes with an "in-tending," or a "tending inwards," a spiritually interiorizing movement, engaging the deepest point of the heart of the believer in the quest for God. What is shared in common is the fundamental aspiration to worship the one and only God — the objective, transcendent, unique, and ineffable Reality; that which is not shared in common is the manner in which that Reality is conceived, and the mode by which that Reality is worshiped: we have here a fusion at the level of the Essence, without any confusion at the level of forms. The dogmas and rituals of each faith remain distinct and thus irreducible, while the summit of the path delineated by dogma and ritual is understood to be one and the same. It might be argued that the degree of ambiguity attaching to Christian worship — worshiping God "through Jesus" — opens such worship up to the charge of polytheism. But one can retort that conceptual ambiguity in terms of reference is trumped by spiritual intentionality in sincere worship; conversely, that which is sincerely intended cannot be invalidated by that which is ambiguously defined. Given that divine reality can never be exhaustively defined, the most one can aim at in this domain is less inadequate conceptions, accompanied by a spirit of humble acknowledgment that the divine reality forever eludes human attempts at comprehension. "*That* there is a God is clear; but *what* He is by essence and nature, this is altogether beyond our comprehension and knowledge," as St. John of Damascus put it.[47]

One can and must accept that there is an irreducible theological in-

---

47. *On the Orthodox Faith*, 1:4; cited by Timothy Ware, *The Orthodox Church*, p. 217.

compatibility between Islamic and Christian conceptions of God, but one need not go further and claim that this incompatibility permits the Muslim theologian to say that Christians worship something other than God, that their worship is a form of polytheism. This would be justified neither by the Qur'ānic discourse pertaining to Christianity taken as a whole, nor by the Prophet's sayings, again, taken as a whole, and particularly in relation to his allowance of Christian worship in the mosque of Medina. Such an act on his part would be unthinkable were this worship to be qualifiable as "polytheistic" in any sense. One can indeed imagine the Prophet receiving Arab polytheist leaders into his mosque, for it is true that the Prophet's mosque at that time was not only a place of worship, it also served as a kind of *dīwān* or court; but one cannot imagine the Prophet inviting any polytheist to pray to his gods in the mosque.

Nonetheless, some Muslim theologians might argue that the Prophet was only being "diplomatic" and "courteous" in allowing the Christians to pray in his mosque, and that one must not draw any theological implications from this act. The argument however backfires, for if the Prophet were willing to go so far, for the sake of diplomacy and courtesy, as to permit "polytheistic" worship to be enacted in his mosque, how much more incumbent is this "diplomacy" and "courtesy" upon his followers, who must, according to the logic of this argument, refrain from characterizing Christian worship as "polytheistic," if only out of a diplomacy and courtesy in emulation of the prophetic example? For Muslims to accuse Christians of engaging in polytheism is, therefore, not only to go much further than the Prophet or the Qur'ān ever went; it also constitutes an implicit criticism of the Prophet for compromising an essential theological principle — distinguishing clearly between *Tawhīd* and *shirk* — for the sake of something so eminently contingent as "diplomacy" or "courtesy."

The metaphysical principle expressed by the Prophet's act can also be discerned in an eschatological event described by the Prophet. The following saying — which exists in slightly different variants, in the most canonical of *hadīth* collections — concerns the possibility of seeing God in the Hereafter. The Muslims are confronted by a theophany of their Lord, whom they do not recognize: "I am your Lord," He says to them. "We seek refuge in God from you," they reply. "We do not associate anything with our Lord." Then God asks them: "Is there any sign (*āya*) between you and Him by means of which you might recognize Him?" They reply in the affirmative, and then "all is revealed," and they all try to prostrate to Him. Finally, as regards this part of the scene, "He transforms Himself into the form in which they saw Him the first time,[48] and He says: 'I am your Lord,' and they reply: 'You are our Lord!'"[49]

Ibn al-ʿArabī and the "God Created in Belief"

The consequences of this remarkable saying are far-reaching. God can appear in forms quite unrecognizable in terms of the beliefs held by Muslims; and if this be true on the Day of Judgment it is equally so in this world. In the Sufi tradition, Ibn al-ʿArabī provides arguably the most compelling commentary on the cognitive implications of this principle. In so doing he also furnishes us with strong grounds for answering in the affirmative the question posed to us in this consultation. The essence of his commentary is that one and the same Reality can take a multitude of forms, hence It must not be confined within the forms of one's own belief. The divinity conceived by the mind is not, and cannot be, the pure Absolute, but is, rather, the "god created in beliefs" *(al-ilāh al-makhlūq fi'l-iʿtiqādāt)*. This "created" god, however, far from being a source of misguidance for the creatures, is itself the consequence of the merciful radiation of the God who loves to be known, in accordance with the well-known saying, cited more by the Sufis than the theologians: "I was a hidden treasure, and I loved to be known." Ibn al-ʿArabī comments on this in many places, but here, the most important aspect of the saying concerns the mercy inherent in the love to be known: "After the Mercy Itself, 'the god created in belief' is the first recipient of Mercy."[50] God is said to have "written mercy" upon His own soul, according to the Qur'ān (6:12, and 6:54). Being Himself the essence of Mercy, the first "form" receiving that mercy is the quality of mercy itself, the fount of radiant creativity. Thereafter, the "god created in belief" receives merciful existentiation, and this refers not just to the diverse modes of theophanic

---

48. The wording here is extremely important: *wa-qad tahawwala fī sūratihi allatī ra'ūhu fīhā awwal marra.*

49. This version of the saying comes in the *Sahīh Muslim* (Cairo: Īsā al-Bābī al-Halabī, n.d), chapter titled "*Maʿrifa tarīq al-ru'yā*" ("knowledge of the way of vision"), vol. 1, p. 94.

50. *Fusūs al-hikam*, translated as *Bezels of Wisdom*, by R. Austin (New York: Paulist Press, 1980), pp. 224-25. For a discussion of this theme of universality in the context of his metaphysical teachings see our *Paths to Transcendence: According to Shankara, Ibn al-Arabi and Meister Eckhart* (Bloomington: World Wisdom, 2006), the chapter on Ibn al-ʿArabī (pp. 69-129).

revelation to humankind, but also to the capacity of each human soul to conceive of God, thus, in a sense, the power to "create" God in one's belief. "Since God is the root of every diversity in beliefs . . . everyone will end up with mercy. For it is He who created them [the diverse beliefs]."[51]

According to this perspective, the various revelations, along with diverse beliefs fashioned thereby, constitute so many ways by which God invites His creatures to participate in His infinitely merciful nature. Recognition of such realities means that it is "improper" to deny God such as He is conceived in the beliefs of others:

> Generally speaking, each man necessarily sticks to a particular creed concerning his Lord. He always goes back to his Lord through his particular creed and seeks God therein. Such a man positively recognizes God only when He manifests Himself to him in the form recognized by his creed. But when He manifests Himself in other forms he denies Him and seeks refuge from Him. In so doing he behaves in an improper way towards Him in fact, even while believing that he is acting politely towards Him. Thus a believer who sticks to his particular creed believes only in a god that he has subjectively posited in his own mind. God in all particular creeds is dependent upon the subjective act of positing on the part of the believers.[52]

In other words, God mercifully and lovingly reveals Himself to His creation in theophanies that cannot but conform themselves to the subjective limitations of the creature; but there is a dynamic interaction between the human subject and the divine Object, between the accidental container and the substantial content: the human is drawn into the divine, to the extent that the conceptually circumscribed form of belief gives way to the spiritual realization of the content of belief. If this spiritual movement or tendency from the form to the essence, from the subject to the object, from the container to the content, does not take place, then one envisages the opposite: the human subjectivization of the divine, the relativization of the Absolute, the individual becoming blinded by the contingent form of his belief from its essential content.

---

51. Cited by William C. Chittick, *The Sufi Path of Knowledge: Ibn al-'Arabī's Metaphysics of Imagination* (Albany: State University of New York Press, 1989), p. 388.

52. Cited by Toshihiko Izutsu, *Sufism and Taoism* (Berkeley: University of California Press, 1983), p. 254 (translation modified).

As mentioned above, the different beliefs are *a priori* determined by the "heart," but the capacity of the heart itself is in turn fashioned by an initial cosmogonic effusion of grace from the merciful Lord. So human subjectivity is itself the result of divine creativity, and cannot therefore intrinsically relativize the Absolute, even while appearing to do so. God not only creates man, but in a sense allows man to create Him, which he does by conceiving of Him and believing in Him and worshiping Him according to the modes determined by the form assumed by his belief. God, however, is truly present and active within that belief — or at least one dimension of divinity is. For Ibn al-ʿArabī distinguishes between the absolute Essence of God — sometimes referred to as *al-Ahad,* the all-exclusive One — and the Lord *(al-Rabb),* also called the "divinity" *(al-ulūhiyya),* or simply the "level" *(al-martaba),* or *al-Wāhid,* the all-inclusive One. These two dimensions of the one and only divinity help us to see that the distinctiveness of the divine qualities is conceivable only at the first degree of Self-manifestation. It is only at this level of theophany that the perfections hidden within the supramanifest "treasure" of the divine Oneness are distinctively affirmed as a plurality; it is only at this level that there is a foreshadowing of the manifestation of the infinite perfections of the all-exclusive One, this anticipation of multiplicity not detracting one iota from its oneness. For the plurality of its perfections is still located at the principial, supramanifest level, that of a oneness which is "all-inclusive," *al-wāhidiyya.* The distinction between these two dimensions of oneness, *al-wāhidiyya* and *al-ahadiyya* (or the oneness of the many, *ahadiyyat al-kathra,* and the oneness of the one, *ahadiyyat al-ahad),* is crucial in the metaphysics of Ibn al-ʿArabī; and what must be stressed about this distinction is that it pertains to the divine nature and nothing else; it refers to two dimensions of oneness within the absolutely indivisible divine nature, one dimension pertaining to the Absolute as such, and the other to the Absolute with its "face" turned towards creation. As we shall see below, this distinction can help us to demonstrate the compatibility between the Trinity, metaphysically or supratheologically conceived, and the principle of *Tawhīd.*

We can only know, and relate to, the names and qualities of the Lord, or the "divinity," or the "level"; but there can be no direct, unmediated relationship between us and the Essence. This is because the Essence has nothing to do with creation; the only possible kind of relationship between the divine Reality and creation is mediated by an intermediary principle, which is the Lord, the "divinity" or the "level": a principle at once divine *and* relative. It is this degree of relativity within divinity that can be conceived, and thus believed in and worshiped. This is the first degree of theophanic Self-determination proper to the Essence, which remains, nonetheless, forever transcendent in relation to all that flows forth from this Self-determination, and *a fortiori,* all that takes place within creation: "It is not correct for the Real and creation to come together in any mode whatsoever in respect of the Essence"; the Real and creation can only be brought into relationship "in respect of the fact that the Essence is described by divinity."[53]

The Essence becoming "described" by divinity means that It is *transcribed* within relativity by this theophany, without in any way sacrificing its immutable transcendence. It is this divinity or Lord that, alone, can be conceived and worshiped. Ibn al-'Arabī expresses this principle in various ways, among which the most striking is the following exegesis of 18:119: "Let him not associate (any) one with his Lord's worship." The immediately apparent meaning of the verse relates to the prohibition of *shirk,* or associating false gods with the true divinity or with the worship of that divinity, but Ibn al-'Arabī makes the "one" in question refer to the Essence, and interprets the verse thus:

> He is not worshiped in respect of His Unity, since Unity contradicts the existence of the worshiper. It is as if He is saying, "What is worshiped is only the 'Lord' in respect of His Lordship, since the Lord brought you into existence. So connect yourself to Him and make yourself lowly before Him, and do not associate Unity with Lordship in worship. . . . For Unity does not know you and will not accept you."[54]

The degree of divinity that can be conceived of, believed in, and worshiped cannot be the pure untrammeled unity of the Essence. There is no room, in this metaphysical unity, for the multiplicity presupposed by creation. To speak of the Creator is to speak of the creature, to speak of the Lord is to speak of the vassal: but the One has no "other" to which it relates; if it did, it would cease to be the Absolute, it would be relativized by its relationship to the relative. We must not, therefore, "associate" Unity with Lordship: in terms of Unity, the creature is a pure nonentity, it is only in relation to the Lord that the creature has any existence, and the *raison*

53. Izutsu, *Sufism and Taoism,* p. 59.
54. Izutsu, *Sufism and Taoism,* p. 244.

d'être of the creature is to worship the Lord whom it can conceive. The One, however, forever evades the conceptualization that is the basis for forming belief. We can conceive that it is, but not what it is. It is for this reason that the Prophet asserted, in various sayings: meditate on the qualities of God, but not on His Essence.[55]

As we shall see with both St. Dionysius and Eckhart, this apophatic approach to the supreme Reality opens up a path that transcends all divergences as regards theological descriptions of God. To continue with this brief exposition of Ibn al-'Arabī's perspective, let us note that despite the transcendence of the One above all beliefs concerning it, God is nonetheless "with every object of belief." This statement evokes the divine utterance: "I am with the opinion My slave has of Me."[56] The word "with" translates *'inda*, which might also be translated as "present within/as/to"[57]: God thus declares that, in a sense, He conforms to whatever form of belief His slave has of him. Ibn al-'Arabī continues: "His [i.e., God's] existence in the conception *(tasawwur)* of him who conceives Him does not disappear when that person's conception changes into another conception. No, He has an existence in this second conception. In the same way, on the Day of Resurrection, he will transmute Himself in self-disclosure from form to form."[58]

Ibn al-'Arabī is here referring back to the principle of the divine capacity to undergo *tahawwul*, according to the prophetic saying cited earlier. What is true of God on the Day of Resurrection is true here and now. Whether it be a case of different individuals, different schools of thought within Islam, or different religions: God is truly present within all these diverse conceptions and beliefs concerning Him, without this resulting in

55. Al-Rāghib al-Isfahānī, a major lexicographer of the Qur'ān, writes in his explanation of the Qur'ānic concept of *fikr*, "meditative thought": "Meditation is only possible in regard to that which can assume a conceptual form *(sūra)* in one's heart. Thus we have the following saying [of the Prophet]: Meditate upon the bounties of God but not on God [Himself, His Essence] for God is above and beyond all possibility of being described in terms of any form *(sūra)*." *Mu'jam mufradāt alfāz al-Qur'ān* (Beirut: Dār al-Fikr, n.d.), p. 398.

56. This is a strongly authenticated *hadīth qudsī*, or divine utterance, transmitted by the Prophet. It is found in Bukhārī, al-Tirmidhī, and Ibn Mājah. See *Forty Hadith Qudsi*, selected and translated by E. Ibrahim and D. Johnson-Davies (Beirut: Dar al-Koran al-Kareem, 1980), p. 78.

57. The translators of the above-mentioned work render the saying as follows: "I am as My servant thinks I am."

58. Chittick, *Sufi Path*, p. 337.

any fundamental contradiction, given the unlimited forms by which God can reveal Himself. What we are given here is a picture of radical relativism, but one that, paradoxically, "proves" the one and only Absolute. For the Absolute is that which transcends all possible powers of conception, and yet immanently and mercifully pervades all those conceptions of Him that stem from authentic divine theophanies. One of the most useful images employed by Ibn al-'Arabī to reconcile the two terms of this paradox is this: water takes on the color of the cup. The cup symbolizes the form of belief, while the water contained therein stands for the Object of belief.

> He who sees the water only in the cup judges it by the property of the cup. But he who sees it simple and noncompound knows that the shapes and colors in which it becomes manifest are the effect of the containers. Water remains in its own definition and reality, whether in the cup or outside it. Hence it never loses the name "water."[59]

In this image, the cup symbolizes the form of the "preparedness" or "receptivity" *(isti'dād)* of a particular belief; the water in the cup symbolizes the theophany that has adapted itself to the form and shape of the belief. The substance and color of water as such is undifferentiated and unique, but it appears to undergo changes of form and color on account of the accidental forms of the receptacles in which it is poured. This recognition enables one to realize that the "water" (or theophanies) in "cups" (or beliefs) other than one's own is just as much "water" as is the water in one's own cup. One can thus affirm the veracity of all beliefs or, rather, all those beliefs whose "cups" contain the water of authentic Revelation, even if these beliefs are also forged by the unavoidable relativity of the creaturely faculty of conception.

This principle is explicitly reaffirmed in the following important passage:

> He who counsels his own soul should investigate during his life in this world, all doctrines concerning God. He should learn from whence each possessor of a doctrine affirms the validity of his doctrine. Once its validity has been affirmed for him in the specific mode in which it is correct for him who upholds it, then he should support it in the case of him who believes in it. He should not deny it or reject it, for he will

59. Chittick, *Sufi Path,* pp. 341-42.

gather its fruit on the Day of Visitation. . . . So turn your attention to what we have mentioned and put it into practice! Then you will give the Divinity its due. . . . For God is exalted high above entering under delimitation. He cannot be tied down by one form rather than another. From here you will come to know the all-inclusiveness of felicity for God's creatures and the all-embracingness of the mercy which covers everything.[60]

In answer to the question, how does one ascertain the "validity" of a doctrine or belief, Ibn al-'Arabī would answer in terms of revelation: those doctrines that clearly derive from or are rooted in a revelation of God are to be accepted. This answer emerges from the following sentence, dealing with the legitimacy of prostration to something "other than God" — as did the angels to Adam, or the family of Joseph to Joseph: "He who prostrates himself to other than God seeking nearness to God *and obeying God* will be felicitous and attain deliverance, but he who prostrates himself to other than God *without God's command* seeking nearness will be wretched" (emphasis added).[61]

Doctrines and beliefs that are man-made are thus clearly rejected — we are far from an "anything goes" attitude that accepts all doctrines as true in an indiscriminate manner. Rather, we are being urged by Ibn al-'Arabī to be open to all receptacles that contain beliefs rooted in divine revelation, and to judge them according to their content, rather than be misled into judging the content according to the accidental properties of the container. What is "accidental" here includes even the dogmas of the different faiths, none of which can claim to exhaust the mystery of that Substance to which they allude.

To affirm only the "God" created within one's belief is thus tantamount to denying Him in all other beliefs: "He who delimits Him denies Him in other than his own delimitation. . . . But he who frees Him from every delimitation never denies Him. On the contrary, he acknowledges Him in every form within which He undergoes self-transmutation."[62] The consequences of this denial will be a diminution in one's receptivity to the loving mercy contained within the beliefs of others. However, attaching

---

60. Chittick, *Sufi Path,* pp. 355-56.
61. Chittick, *Sufi Path,* p. 365.
62. Chittick, *Sufi Path,* pp. 339-40. See our *Paths to Transcendence* for further discussion of these themes in the context of the quest for transcendent realization, according to these three mystics.

oneself only to the "water" within one's own cup still results in mercy, given that the theophanic form is still a true theophany; it is God and nothing but God, even if the form assumed by God be extrinsically limited by the form of one's belief: there is an absoluteness of content, combined with a relativity of the container, but that absoluteness is not relativized by the container. Rather, what is excluded by the container is the infinite forms of theophany filling the containers of other beliefs. In other words, it is not the case that God is relativized by the specificity of one's belief, by the limited container; rather, the relativity of the human belief is displaced by the absoluteness of its own content, in the measure that this content is realized through spiritual assimilation, and not just conceived by rational thought. For then one perceives — or drinks — water as such, the substance of which is identical to that contained in all other containers. So the very absoluteness of the content of one's realized belief leads to an assimilation of the infinitude proper to that absoluteness. "Drinking" the water within one's own cup means drinking water as such, and thus, in principle, one has drunk the same substance as that which is contained in all the other cups. As we said at the outset, one believes in God as such and not such and such a god.

Even if this total realization is not attained, the believer will nonetheless benefit from his capacity to recognize God in beliefs other than his own, for he has a glimpse of the felicity that flows from the unrestricted beatific vision of God in all His forms. The beatific vision experienced by the believer in the Hereafter will conform to the nature of his conception and attitude towards God in the here-below. This is clearly asserted by Ibn al-ʿArabī in the course of describing the "share" accorded to the highest saint: he enjoys the felicity that is the fruit of all forms of belief held by the faithful of the different religions, because he recognizes their correspondence to real aspects of the divine nature.[63] This direct and plenary participation in the felicity that is contained within the forms of beliefs concerning God is thus seen to be a reality already in this life — a prefiguration of the higher celestial states.

Thus, Ibn al-ʿArabī urges the believer to make himself receptive to all forms of religious belief both for the sake of objective veracity — that is, "the true knowledge of the reality" that God is immanent within all forms of His Self-revelation — and in the interests of one's posthumous state — the "great benefit" that accrues to the soul in the Hereafter in proportion

---

63. See M. Chodkiewicz, *Le Sceau des Saints* (Paris: Gallimard, 1986), p. 73.

to the universality of the knowledge of God it has attained on earth. The vision that results from this openness to the diversity of theophanies within the forms of different beliefs is beautifully expressed in the most famous lines from Ibn al-'Arabī's poetic masterpiece, *Tarjumān al-ashwāq*:

> My heart has become capable of every form:
> it is a pasture for gazelles and a convent for Christian monks,
> And a temple for idols and the pilgrim's Ka'ba,
> and the tables of the Torah and the book of the Koran.
> I follow the religion of Love: whatever way Love's camels take,
> that is my religion and my faith.[64]

It is clear that in these lines Ibn al-'Arabī is not affirming that the forms mentioned are all equally legitimate religious forms; only that they are all, *qua* forms, equally manifestations of the divine reality. He is making an ontological and not specifically religious affirmation. Everything manifested in being is a manifestation of God, since God is being; on this basis, he interprets the verse: "Thy Lord has decreed that you shall not worship any but Him" (17:23) as a descriptive statement rather than as a normative injunction, for God is "identical with everything toward which there is poverty and which is worshiped."[65] Everything that is worshiped is therefore divine, but as regards the specifically religious criterion for authentic worship, this, as seen above, is derived upon the principle of God's scriptural revelations, which are concrete and specific, not on the divine self-disclosures within the domain of manifestation, which are universal and inescapable.

Finally, let us look at the remarkable interpretation given by Ibn al-'Arabī to one of his own lines of poetry in this work. This gives us one possible way of understanding the meaning of the Christian Trinity from a mystical Muslim perspective. The line in the poem is as follows: "My Beloved is three although He is One, even as the Persons are made one Person in essence." The interpretation given by the poet himself: "Number does not beget multiplicity in the Divine Substance, as the Christians declare that the Three Persons of the Trinity are One God, and as the Qur'ān de-

---

64. *The Tarjuman Al-Ashwaq,* trans. R. A. Nicholson (London: Royal Asiatic Society, 1978), p. 52.

65. Cited by W. Chittick, "Towards Sainthood: States and Stations," in *Les Illuminations de la Mecque,* ed. M. Chodkiewicz (Paris: Sindbad, 1988), p. 319.

clares: 'Call upon God or call on the Merciful; however ye invoke Him, it is well, for to Him belong the most beautiful Names (17:110).'"[66]

The most beautiful Names of God, *al-asmā᾽ al-husnā*, can be seen as the archetypes of all possible modes of theophany, and thereby, of the diverse — even contradictory — beliefs of God fashioned by those theophanic modes of self-revelation. The names are diverse, referring to the different aspects of the Named; beliefs fashioned by the revelation of those names are thus likewise inescapably diverse, but all the beliefs are nonetheless at one in the supreme Object of faith. Ibn al-ʿArabī unreservedly identifies the three Persons of the Trinity as three aspects or "names" of the one Essence, thus resolving multiplicity within unity in a manner that is analogous to that by means of which the ninety-nine "names" refer to but one Essence in Islam. For "number does not beget multiplicity in the divine Substance." As we shall see below, this is a mirror image of what Eckhart says about the Trinity, about number within the divinity, and about "a hundred" Persons within the one God. Both Eckhart and Ibn al-ʿArabī situate plurality within the divine nature on a plane that is below that of the Essence, a plane that pertains to the relationship between the Essence and the domain of manifestation. To speak of "relationship" is thus ineluctably to speak of relativity, and it is on this plane of relativity — still within the divine nature itself, but relativity nonetheless — that one can ascribe plurality to God. The Essence, however, transcends this relativity and is "one" not in any numerical sense of unity that can be distinguished, on the same plane of number, from plurality; for then we would still be on the plane of relativity, asserting one "unit" or thing as opposed to other similarly located units or things. Rather, the Essence is one in a properly metaphysical sense, a sense that goes beyond *physis* or nature, understanding by nature all that which pertains to the created order, and number evidently pertains to this order. Number as applied to God must then be applied in a consciously metaphysical manner: if one is to speak of God in terms of the contingent category of number, then one should assert that God is indeed "one," for, on the plane of number, "one" is the most adequate symbol by which the Absolute can be described.[67]

66. Chittick, "Towards Sainthood," p. 70.

67. As Frithjof Schuon writes, in his irrefutable critique — and also inspiring interpretation — of the dogma of the Trinity: "Only Unity as such can be a definition of the Absolute; in the realm of number, unity alone represents an element of absoluteness, as does

Spiritual receptivity to the realization of the Essence is deepened by the capacity to conceive of the inescapably limited nature of *all* conceptions: the intrinsically inconceivable nature of ultimate Reality can be realized, to one degree or another, in spiritual vision, that vision which arises in proportion to the effacement of the individual *(fanā')*. This shift from conceptual limitation to spiritual vision is well expressed by Ibn al-'Arabī in relation to Moses' quest to see God. Ibn al-'Arabī records the following dialogue he had with Moses in the course of his spiritual ascent through the heavens:

> [I said to him] . . . you requested the vision [of God], while the Messenger of God [Muhammad] said that "not one of you will see his Lord until he dies."
>
> So he said: "And it was just like that: when I asked Him for the vision, He answered me, so that 'I fell down stunned' (Q 7, 143). Then I saw Him in my [state of] being stunned." I said: "While (you were) dead?" He replied: "While (I was) dead. . . . I did not see God until I had died."[68]

This is the consummation of the apophatic path: "extinction within contemplation" *(al-fanā' fi'l-mushāhada)*, this being precisely the title of one of Ibn al-'Arabī's most explicit treatises on the theme of *fanā'*.[69] As we shall see in a moment, the similarities between this perspective and those of both St. Dionysius and Meister Eckhart are striking.

Christian Apophaticism and Superessential Identity

The perspective of Ibn al-'Arabī, we would argue, is mirrored in the apophatic tradition of mystical theology within Christianity. It is in this tradition that all dogmatic formulations of the ultimate Reality are seen as

---

the point or the centre in space, and the instant or the present in time. . . ." This is from the essay titled "Evidence and Mystery" in his *Logic and Transcendence*, p. 91. For another compelling interpretation of the Trinity, see Schuon's *Understanding Islam* (Bloomington: World Wisdom, 1994), p. 53.

68. Cited by James W. Morris, "The Spiritual Ascension: Ibn 'Arabī and the *Mi'rāj*," *Journal of the American Oriental Society* 108 (1988): 375.

69. See Michel Valsan's translation, *Le Livre de l'Extinction dans la Contemplation* (Paris: Les Éditions de l'Oeuvre, 1984).

falling short of adequately explaining or describing it. As with Ibn al-'Arabī's "god created in beliefs," mystics of this tradition insist on the need to transcend all conceptual expressions, and the very source of those concepts, the mind itself, in order to glimpse with the eye of the heart, and finally to realize in the depths of one's spirit, the ineffable mystery of God. We would argue that it is through understanding this process of radical deconstruction at the conceptual level, grasped as the prelude to an "unthinkable" spiritual "reconstruction" at the transcendent level, that the oneness of the God believed in by Christians and Muslims stands out most clearly. For if the mind and all that it can conceive are transcended by the spiritual realization of That which is inconceivable, then *a fortiori* all designations of the Ineffable are likewise transcended, even those designations that form the core of the Trinitarian dogma.

Let us note first of all the importance of the following point made by Vladimir Lossky about this tradition of "thought" in general: it is one in which thought itself is subordinated to "being," to an existential transformation of the soul:

> Apophaticism is not necessarily a theology of ecstasy. It is, above all, an attitude of mind which refuses to form concepts about God. Such an attitude utterly excludes all abstract and purely intellectual theology which would adapt the mysteries of the wisdom of God to human ways of thoughts. It is an existential attitude which involves the whole man: there is no theology apart from experience; it is necessary to change, to become a new man. To know God one must draw near to Him. No one who does not follow the path of union with God can be a theologian. The way of the knowledge of God is necessarily the way of deification. . . . Apophaticism is, therefore, a criterion: the sure sign of an attitude of mind conformed to truth. In this sense all true theology is fundamentally apophatic.[70]

Further on in this seminal text, Lossky refers to the ultimate function of the dogma of the Trinity: "The dogma of the Trinity is a cross for human ways of thought."[71] We understand this to mean that the dogma of the Trinity is not intended to function as an "explanation" or "description" of God; rather, it is a means of thinking the unthinkable in order to efface

70. Lossky, *Mystical Theology*, p. 39.
71. Lossky, *Mystical Theology*, p. 66.

all thought within the mystery that is intrinsically incommunicable. This principle is brought home clearly by St. Dionysius in his prayer to the Deity "above all essence, knowledge and goodness" at the very beginning of his treatise *The Mystical Theology*: ". . . direct our path to the ultimate summit of Thy mystical Lore, most incomprehensible, most luminous and most exalted, where the pure, absolute and immutable mysteries of theology are veiled in the dazzling obscurity of the secret Silence, outshining all brilliance with the intensity of their Darkness."[72]

The purpose of defining the ultimate reality in terms of darkness, and as that which is even "beyond being," is not simply to shroud that reality in utter, impenetrable obscurity, but rather to precipitate receptivity to that reality by showing the inability of the human mind in and of itself to attain comprehension of, or union with, that reality. It is the contrast between ultimate reality — as utter Darkness — and mental abstraction — apparent light — that is in question. He continues, addressing his disciple:

> Do thou, dear Timothy, in the diligent exercise of mystical contemplation, leave behind the senses and the operations of the intellect, and all things sensible and intellectual, and all things in the world of being and non-being, that thou mayest arise by unknowing towards the union, as far as is attainable, with Him who transcends all being and all knowledge. For by the unceasing and absolute renunciation of thyself and of all things, thou mayest be borne on high, through pure and entire self-abnegation, into the superessential Radiance of the Divine Darkness.

He then refers to the "transcendental First Cause," and criticizes those who identify God with "the images which they fashion after various designs." This resonates deeply with Ibn al-'Arabī's image of the cup and the water. The similarity between the two perspectives is deepened when we read that this transcendent Reality "reveals Himself in His naked Truth to those alone who pass beyond all that is pure and impure, and ascend above the summit of holy things, and who, leaving behind them all divine light and sound and heavenly utterances, plunge into the Darkness where truly dwells, as the Scriptures declare, that One Who is beyond all."[73]

---

72. Dionysius the Areopagite, *Mystical Theology and the Celestial Hierarchies* (Fintry, UK: The Shrine of Wisdom Press, 1965), p. 19.

73. Dionysius the Areopagite, *Mystical Theology*, p. 21.

This One is evidently beyond any conceivable notion of threeness — but it is also, as we shall see, equally beyond any conceivable notion of oneness. First, let us note that, like Ibn al-ʿArabī, Dionysius uses Moses' quest for the vision of God to bring home the point that God cannot be seen, but He can be realized. God cannot be seen because "the divinest and highest things seen by the eyes or contemplated by the mind are but the symbolical expressions of those that are immediately beneath Him Who is above all." It is only through being plunged into the Darkness, and after "all his reasoning powers" have been silenced, that the soul can be "united by his highest faculty to Him who is wholly unknowable; thus by knowing nothing, he knows That which is beyond his knowledge."[74]

We are reminded here of what Ibn al-ʿArabī said in relation to the Lord/divinity/level: it is that aspect of Reality which, in contrast to the Essence, *can* be conceived; it is that degree of being, beneath the Essence, to which belief and worship are directed and proportioned. Likewise for St. Dionysius, vision, conception, and contemplation pertain only to the penultimate ontological degree, not to ultimate Reality: "the divinest and highest things seen by the eyes or contemplated by the mind are but the *symbolical expressions* of those that are *immediately beneath* Him Who is above all." All doctrines and dogmas, even those reaching up to the "divinest and highest" cannot even be regarded as symbols of ultimate Reality itself; they can only symbolize what is "immediately beneath Him." The function of the symbols, then, is to induce receptivity to that which cannot even be adequately symbolized let alone explained or described by concepts. We would propose, on the basis of this apophatic understanding of symbols, that the Trinity constitutes just such a symbol of penultimate Reality; it cannot be applied to the ultimate Reality, for this latter cannot in any way be symbolized.

If all visible and intelligible forms are alike "symbolical expressions" of the penultimate Reality, they must therefore be "seen through," just as one must see through the "cup" of one's belief to the water it "contains." This capacity to appreciate the symbolic nature of one's beliefs, and indeed of one's entire conceptual apparatus, is the prerequisite for taking the plunge into that Oneness which is inconceivable, being beyond even the notion of oneness. In this light, the essential nature of the divinity affirmed by Christians and Muslims can be intuited as one and the same Reality, that Reality which can only extrinsically be conceived of or symbol-

---

74. Dionysius the Areopagite, *Mystical Theology*, pp. 21-22.

ized. The most faithful or least inadequate means of alluding to this Reality, however, is not through affirmation, but through radical denial. The Transcendent One is described as not being "one or oneness . . . nor sonship nor fatherhood."[75]

Both the Christian dogma of the Trinity and the Muslim doctrine of *Tawhīd* are here being challenged — as *concepts*. The ultimate Reality cannot be described in terms of number, nor *a fortiori*, in terms of any dualistic relationship such as is implied by "fatherhood" and "sonship." Both the idea of oneness and that of trinity are alike to be grasped as symbolic of the threshold of Reality, and are not to be taken literally as definitions of that threshold, or, still less, as definitions of the Essence of that Reality. The first testimony of Islam, *lā ilāha illa'Llāh*, "no divinity but God," can be metaphysically understood to refer to the apophatic principle being described here: no conceivable divinity, only the inconceivable Absolute. One can conceive that the Absolute is, but one cannot conceive exactly what it is. It can be intuited as absolute Reality, the source of all being and existents, or as absolute Goodness, the source of all felicity and love, or as absolute Consciousness, source of all wisdom and knowledge, but what the *absoluteness* of these qualities really means cannot be put into words.[76]

---

75. Dionysius the Areopagite, *Mystical Theology*, p. 29.

76. We have elaborated upon this theme in our *Paths to Transcendence*. The three mystics studied in that work are at one in affirming that while the Absolute is indeed ineffable and incommunicable in its essence, it reveals something of its nature in the ultimate spiritual realization, and that "something" is described by each of these mystics in strikingly similar terms. In this, we believe, there lies an answer to the questions posed in Denys Turner's excellent paper in this volume, "Christians, Muslims, and the Name of God: Who Owns It, and How Would We Know?" The crux of his position is summed up in this sentence: "For the absolute unknowableness of 'ultimate reality' eliminates all content on which any criteria of sameness and difference can get a grip." On this basis, Turner argues that there is no "apophatic solution" to the question of whether or not Muslims and Christians worship the same God. We would argue, however, that for the mystics we studied the impossibility of acquiring full cognitive knowledge of ultimate Reality paradoxically goes hand in hand with spiritual realization of that reality. This realization produces a certain degree of knowledge of Reality, such knowledge being the trace or, to use Shankara's term, reflection *(abhasa)*, of Reality left within the consciousness of the mystic after his return to "normal" modes of awareness. One who only sees the sun as it is reflected in a mirror will know *something* of the nature of the sun, but nothing of its true dimensions in space. Likewise, the mystic, upon the return to normal awareness, will be able to speak of the reflected image of the reality attained in the moment or state of enlightenment, but cannot convey anything of the "dimensions" — absolute, infinite, perfect — of that reality as it truly is. As Ibn al-'Arabī writes: "Gnostics cannot impart their spiritual states to other men; they can only indicate

There is therefore something communicable about the nature of the Absolute, as well as something incommunicable; it is ineffable in its essence and yet reveals something of that essence to the prophets, saints, sages, and mystics. It might be spiritually glimpsed by the "eye of the heart" of the spiritual seeker, an "eye" whose opening is predicated upon some degree of self-effacement, initially, and "extinction," ultimately. In the wake of this vision, however, it is still impossible to adequately describe in words the Reality glimpsed. As al-Ghazālī put it: "He who has attained the mystic state need do no more than say: 'Of the things I do not remember, what was, was; think it good; do not ask an account of it.'"[77]

Eckhartian Trinity and Metaphysical Tawhīd

Let us now turn to Meister Eckhart, and look in particular at the daring manner in which the Trinity is articulated in the wake of the realization of the Absolute. His exposition of the Trinity has the merit of rendering explicit some of the key premises that may be implicit in the assertion by Christians that the Muslims do believe in the same God as themselves, even if they, the Muslims, deny the Trinity: they believe in the Essence of that Divinity which can "assume" dogmatically, and at a lower ontological degree, the aspect of threeness. It also has the considerable merit of showing Muslims that there is a presentation of the Trinity that not only harmonizes with *Tawhīd*, but indeed brings to light dimensions of *Tawhīd* in a manner comparable to the greatest of the mystical sages of Islam who have asserted, quite paradoxically, that the *concept* of "monotheism" can be a veil over the One, just as much as polytheism is. That is, it helps the Muslim to transform a dogmatic and formal conception of oneness into an existential, spiritual, and transformative awareness of that which is beyond being and thus, *a fortiori*, infinitely beyond the realm of number.

This, indeed, is the ontological shift of consciousness that the Sufis insist on: God is one, not just in the sense of being "not two" or "not multiple," but in the sense of excluding all otherness. The theological affirmation of one God is transformed into a spiritual realization that there is but

---

them symbolically to those who have begun to experience the like." Quoted by R. A. Nicholson in *The Mystics of Islam* (London: G. Bell, 1914), p. 103 (translation modified).

77. Al-Ghazālī is citing a saying from Ibn al-Muʻtazz in his autobiographical work *al-Munqidh min al-dalāl* ("Deliverance from error"), trans. Montgomery Watt, p. 61.

a unique reality, which is outwardly differentiated by virtue of its own infinite radiance. To think otherwise, for the Sufis, is to fall into a "hidden" polytheism or *shirk*.

Before addressing directly the Trinity, it is worth noting that Eckhart's approach to thought generally coincides precisely with that of Dionysius and Ibn al-ʿArabī. All mentally articulated attributes fall short of "describing" the divine reality: "It is its nature to be without nature. To think of goodness or wisdom or power dissembles the essence and dims it in thought. The mere thought obscures essence. . . . For goodness and wisdom and whatever may be attributed to God are all admixtures to God's naked essence: for all admixture causes alienation from essence."[78]

Its nature is "without nature," that is, it is devoid of any specific nature, or attributes that can be adequately expressed in human language; one must not relativize the divine reality by equating it with any attributes that are susceptible to mental articulation. It does possess these attributes, intrinsically, but it also transcends them, and this is the key point: it is this transcendence of every conceivable attribute that makes it the Absolute. The Absolute possesses all positive attributes, but also transcends them: one is reminded here of the Ashʿarite formula: "the attributes are not God," for the Absolute transcends all attributes; but "the attributes are not other than God," for the Absolute possesses all attributes, and that which is possessed by the Absolute must be one with it, on pain of violating the divine simplicity, and attributing divisible parts to the Absolute.

Eckhart's insistence that our conception of God be shorn of any "nature" or attribute is echoed in the following words of ʿAlī b. Abī Ṭālib, the cousin and son-in-law of the Prophet, fourth caliph of Islam, and first Imam of the Shiʾa Muslims.[79] This is how he comments on the meaning of *ikhlās*, literally "making pure," referring to the purification of one's conception of God:

> The perfection of purification *(ikhlās)* is to divest Him of all attributes
> — because of the testimony of every attribute that it is other than the

78. *Meister Eckhart: Sermons and Treatises*, trans. M. O'C Walshe (Dorset: Element Books, 1979), vol. 2, pp. 32 and 39.

79. He is aptly described by Frithjof Schuon as the "esoteric representative of Islam *par excellence*." See his *The Transcendent Unity of Religions*, trans. Peter Townsend (London: Faber & Faber, 1953), p. 59. See our *Justice and Remembrance: Introducing the Spirituality of Imam ʿAlī* (London: I. B. Tauris, 2006) for discussion of some of the major themes articulated by this seminal figure of nascent Islam.

object of attribution, and because of the testimony of every such object that it is other than the attribute. So whoever ascribes an attribute to God — glorified be He! — has conjoined Him [with something else] and whoever so conjoins Him has made Him two-fold, and whoever makes Him two-fold has fragmented Him, and whoever thus fragments Him is ignorant of Him.[80]

God of course possesses attributes — the ninety-nine "names" of God being the names of these attributes. Imam ʿAlī clearly is not denying the reality of these attributes as such, for earlier in the sermon cited above, he affirms that God's attributes have "no defined limit." They can have no limit because the attributes are ontologically identical to the Essence as such, and have no self-subsisting reality apart from that Essence. One can identify the attributes with the Essence, but not vice versa: it is an act of *shirk* to identify the Essence either with Its own attributes or, still worse, with our understanding of these attributes. Thus, Eckhart's view of the Absolute as transcending all mental conceptions, specific nature, and even (as we shall see in a moment) the Trinity, can easily be read by a Muslim as rooted in the avoidance of subtle *shirk,* and as a commentary on the meaning of the first testimony of Islam, *no divinity but God.*

This is particularly clear when we look at the way in which Eckhart deals with the question of God's "being." For he stresses in many places that God is "beyond Being," and thus transcends all possibility of being described by the attributes proper to Being. God, he says, is as high above being as the highest angel is above the lowest ant.[81] "When I have said God is not a being and is above being, I have not thereby denied Him being: rather I have exalted it in Him. If I get copper in gold, it is there . . . in a nobler mode than it is in itself."[82] The denial, then, of the specific, conceivable attributes of God — including even that most indeterminate and universal attribute, Being itself — means an exaltation of all of these attributes in their undifferentiated essence. This appears to be identical to what Imam ʿAlī means when he negates the divine attributes, on the one hand, and sublimates them on the other. The attributes are more fully and really themselves in the divine oneness than they are in their own specificity, and *a fortiori* in the mental conceptions we have of them. So the denial

---

80. Cited in *The Transcendent Unity of Religions,* p. 208.
81. *Meister Eckhart,* vol. 2, pp. 150-51.
82. *Meister Eckhart,* vol. 2, pp. 150-51.

of the attributes is a denial on the purely mental plane; it is not a denial of their intrinsic substance: conceptual apophasis paves the way for an eminently positive opening to the transcendent substance of the attributes.[83] This substance is one, but it is outwardly articulated in conformity with the differentiated planes upon which its inner infinitude outwardly unfolds. This leads to the following important point pertaining to the nonnumerical nature of the Trinity:

> For anyone who could grasp distinctions without number and quantity, a hundred would be as one. Even if there were a hundred Persons in the Godhead, a man who could distinguish without number and quantity would perceive them only as one God . . . (he) knows that three Persons are one God.[84]

This echoes the point made earlier by Ibn al-ʿArabī: "Number does not beget multiplicity in the divine Substance." God can relate to multiplicity in a variety of ways, but this does not introduce multiplicity into the divine nature; the multiplicity comes from the created or manifested realm: from the world, not from God. But for both Eckhart and Ibn al-ʿArabī, the level of divinity that can assume multiple relations with the realm of relativity is itself perforce relative; it is a level or degree of divinity that is transcended by the Essence of divinity. Thus, this Essence — Eckhart's "Godhead" — transcends all conceivable distinctions. All that can be said of it, provisionally, is that it is absolutely one. Mental conception — and thus all dogma predicated thereupon — is incapable of expressing the reality of God, and yet one has to make an effort to conceive of the divine Essence as pure and untrammeled unity. However, even the conception of oneness is tainted by its very form as a conception: "The mere thought dims the essence." One is thus left with the task of conceiving of the One while at the same time knowing that this conception is inescapably flawed: one has to conceive oneness by spiritually piercing the veil of that very conception. As mentioned earlier: one has to conceive of That which is inconceivable; for it is possible to conceive *that* it is, but impossi-

---

83. One is reminded here of a cognitive principle within the school of Advaita Vedanta: "That which cannot be expressed is expressed through false attribution and subsequent denial *(adhyaropa-apavada)*." It should be noted that the Sanskrit *apavada* is cognate with the Greek *apophasis*. See our *Paths to Transcendence*, pp. 2-8.

84. *Meister Eckhart*, vol. 1, p. 217.

ble to conceive *what* it is. It is a "something" as he says in the passage be-low, "which is neither this nor that."

> So truly one and simple is this citadel, so mode and power transcend-ing is this solitary One, that neither power nor mode can gaze into it, nor even God Himself! . . . God never looks in there for one instant, in so far as He exists in modes and in the properties of His Persons . . . this One alone lacks all mode and property . . . for God to see inside it would cost Him all His divine names and personal properties: all these He must leave outside. . . . But only in so far as He is one and indivisi-ble [can He do this]: in this sense He is neither Father, Son nor Holy Ghost and yet is a something which is neither this nor that.[85]

This metaphysical perspective, clearly indicating the relativity of the ontological plane upon which the Trinity is conceivable, can help Muslims to see that belief in the Trinity does not necessarily imply any compromise as regards the absolute oneness of God; indeed, the sensitive Muslim might come to see the Trinity as a legitimate doctrine accounting for the mystery of God's self-revelation, becoming thereby analogous to the doctrine of the divine names and attributes in Islam. The Persons, like the divine at-tributes in Islam, are identical to the Essence, which is absolute simplicity; but the converse is not true: the Essence is not exhaustively identifiable with any of the Persons. Just as the Persons are distinguished from each other in terms of origin, otherwise being equal in all respects *qua* nature or substance, so the attributes are distinguished from each other in terms of their specific properties, but are equal to each other *qua* Essence: each at-tribute is identical to the Absolute, the object of attribution. In both cases, there is an outward differentiation that does not infringe upon an inward identity, or unicity of substance. The "names" are distinguished in terms of the specific, hence exclusive, properties they denote, but they are also in-distinguishable by virtue of their common root, the Essence. Each name is thus identical to the Essence, in one respect, and distinct therefrom in an-other; as being identical to the Essence, each name is thus identical to every other name. This view of the relationship between the names and the Es-

---

85. *Meister Eckhart,* vol. 1, p. 76. One might note here that Nicholas of Cusa says something very similar. He writes that in His ineffable infinitude, God cannot be described as "one or three or good or wise or Father or Son or Holy Spirit." Rather, God "infinitely ex-cels and precedes all such names." This is from his *Cribratio Alkorani,* p. 88, as cited by Miroslav Volf in *Allah: A Christian Response* (New York: HarperCollins, 2011), p. 51.

sence in Islamic metaphysics can be seen to correspond to the relationship between the Persons and the Godhead in Eckhartian metaphysics. According to Eckhart, the three Persons are identical to each other only at the transcendent level of Beyond-Being, the level that transcends the level of Being or divinity upon which the Persons are distinct as Persons.

One of the clearest expressions of the distinction between the level of the Trinity and the level of the pure Absolute is given by Eckhart when he speaks of the soul being borne up in the Persons, according to the power of the Father, the wisdom of the Son, and the goodness of the Holy Ghost — these three being the modes of "work" proper to the Persons.[86] He goes on to say that it is only above all this "work" that "the pure absoluteness of free being" is to be found; the Persons, as such, are "suspended in being." Here, we have a double lesson: not only is the Trinity relativized in the face of the pure Absolute, it is also rendered conceivable as the deployment of the divine graces by which the soul attains spiritual realization. It is made subordinate to pure or absolute being, on the one hand; and, on the other, it is grasped as the deployment of divine power, wisdom, and goodness which, alone, carry the soul towards its goal and its source, to that "place where the soul grasps the Persons in the very indwelling of being from which they never emerged."

The Persons "never emerged" from the "indwelling of being," because that "indwelling of being" is nothing other than Beyond-Being, or the Godhead, and the essential reality of the Persons "resides" in that Essence; now their essential reality is their true reality — their apparent "emergence" therefrom, *qua* distinct Persons, is just that: an appearance. We are reminded here of what Ibn al-'Arabī says about the divine Names having two connotations: "The first connotation is God Himself Who is what is named, the second that by which one Name is distinguished from another"; so, on the one hand, "the Name is the Reality," while on the other hand, "it is the imagined Reality."[87] More explicitly, as regards the apparent

---

86. *Meister Eckhart*, vol. 2, pp. 174-75. In terms of strict Trinitarian dogma this interpretation might be regarded as depriving the Persons of their full divinity, by ascribing to them only one particular "work" or divine quality. All three Persons, so it might be argued, do all kinds of "work," as each of them is as much God as the other two Persons are, distinguishable one from the other only as regards the single characteristic defining their Personhood: "begetting" for the Father, "being begotten" for the Son, and "proceeding" for the Spirit.

87. Cited by Ralph Austin, *The Bezels of Wisdom* (New York: Paulist Press, 1980), p. 125.

reality of the Names: "The Names in their multiplicity are but relations which are of a non-existent nature."[88]

So, for both Eckhart and Ibn al-ʿArabī, the pure Absolute is identified in terms of an essential oneness that precedes — not so much temporally as ontologically — the degree of being at which any distinctions become discernible. When Eckhart says that the Persons as such are "suspended" at the level of being, this is another way of saying that the Persons "boil over" *(bullitio)* from Beyond-Being into being, from the unique Godhead into and as the Trinitarian God.[89] However, the Trinitarian God is not something other than the Godhead: it is, to paraphrase Ibn al-ʿArabī, the Essence "described" by divinity. It is the oneness of the one *(ahadiyyat al-ahad)* becoming discernible as the oneness of the many *(ahadiyyat al-kathra)*:[90] that

---

88. Cited by Izutsu, *Sufism and Taoism*, p. 161. In referring to the Names as "relations" one thinks of St. Thomas Aquinas's doctrine of the Persons: they, too, are called by St. Thomas "relations" — but he would most likely have problems defining these relations as being "nonexistent." He may accept, however, the argument that they are not "existential," in the sense of "standing apart" from God's *Esse* (Being): they are "nonexistent" because absolutely identical with God's *Esse*, subsisting above all contingent things, all "existents," and are thus "supraexistent." This is similar to Ibn al-ʿArabī's view in one respect, but quite different in another: for Ibn al-ʿArabī, the Names are nonexistent *(ʿadam)* only in their aspect of specificity, hence exclusivity — the fact that in one respect each Name is distinct from and thus excludes all others — because nonexistence is the defining feature of this exclusivity proper to multiplicity. In another respect, however, the Names are real: they are real insofar as they are identical to the Named, the Essence, pure *wujūd* (Being), which is absolutely one, and absolutely universal: absolutely unspecifiable, or nondelimited, and yet also, not delimited by this nondelimitation. "Do not declare Him nondelimited and thus delimited by being distinguished from delimitation!" he warns us: "For if He is distinguished then He is delimited by His nondelimitation. And if He is delimited by His nondelimitation, then He is not He." Cited by Chittick, *Sufi Path*, p. 112. Cf. Denys Turner's illuminating discussion of the meaning of God as *esse indistinctum* (indistinct Being) in Eckhart's perspective, *The Darkness of God: Negativity in Christian Mysticism* (Cambridge: Cambridge University Press, 1995), pp. 162-67.

89. One of Eckhart's boldest claims is to be identified with the undifferentiated Godhead in his uncreated essence. To quote Turner's summary of Eckhart's claims: ". . . not merely does the Father give birth to me in the Son, before all that I was in the Godhead in its absolute, primitive oneness, a oneness which 'precedes' all the differentiations of the Trinity of Persons, that 'seething and boiling' or *bullitio* . . . my existence in the Godhead is beyond all distinctions, in the undifferentiated oneness of the Godhead, it cannot be distinct from the Godhead as such. Therefore I existed in the Godhead *before God*, in God's very 'own ground.' If I was there in that ground at the birth of the Trinity, *a fortiori* I was there before my own creation." *The Darkness of God*, p. 145.

90. "In respect of His Self, God possesses the Unity of the One, but in respect of His Names, He possesses the Unity of the many." Cited by Chittick, *Sufi Path*, p. 337.

which is distinct and discernible as a plurality in the latter is nothing but the initial, metaphysical prefiguration of the perfections that are hidden and undifferentiated in the former. Both Ibn al-'Arabī and Eckhart, then, reveal the inadequacy of *all* mental conceptions of divine unity in the face of the overflowing infinitude of the One. For the purely conceptual affirmation of God's oneness smacks of *shirk* in the measure that it implies that God's oneness is a "countable" or numerical one, that God is simply one unit among other similar units. Imam 'Alī expresses this principle in the following saying. He is asked about the meaning of God's oneness, and refers first to the error of the person "who says 'one' and has in mind the category of numbers. Now this is not permissible, for that which has no second does not enter into the category of numbers."[91]

This statement resonates deeply with the following words of Eckhart:

> One is the negation of the negation and a denial of the denial. All creatures have a negation in themselves: one negates by not being the other . . . but God negates the negation: He is one and negates all else, for outside of God nothing is. All creatures are in God, and are His very Godhead, which means plenitude. . . . God alone has oneness. Whatever is number depends on one, and one depends on nothing. God's riches and wisdom and truth are all absolutely one in God: it is not one, it is oneness.[92]

Referring to the nonnumerical oneness of God as being "that which has no second" is Imam 'Alī's way of referring to the unique reality of God, outside of whom "nothing is," as Eckhart's formulation has it. Similarly, Imam 'Alī's negation of the attributes, and his identification of them all with the simplicity of the divine Essence, is expressed by Eckhart's insistence that God's "riches and wisdom and truth are all absolutely one in God"; and Eckhart's correction of himself, "it is not one, it is oneness," can be read as a deliberate encouragement to his listeners to shift their consciousness from a static numerical conception of unity, standing opposed to an equally static conception of multiplicity, to a dynamic spiritual conception of the eternal integration of multiplicity within unity and the overflowing of the inner riches of that unity within multiplicity. This re-

91. *A Shi'ite Anthology,* ed. and trans. William C. Chittick (n.p.: Muhammadi Trust of Great Britain and Northern Ireland, 1981), p. 37.
92. *Meister Eckhart,* vol. 2, pp. 339 and 341.

ciprocal integration is one aspect of metaphysical *Tawhīd,* and is referred to by the Sufis in terms of "the multiple One" *(al-wāhid al-kathīr)* and the "unique multiplicity" *(al-kathīr al-wāḥid).*[93]

God alone is absolute Reality, for both of these mystical authorities, and this sole reality is at once all-exclusive, by virtue of its ineffable transcendence, and all-inclusive, by virtue of its inescapable immanence. The "negation of negation" is tantamount to pure affirmation, but affirmation not of a countable oneness, rather, of an all-inclusive oneness, within which all conceivable multiplicity is eternally comprised. Imam ʿAlī's way of expressing Eckhart's "negation of negation" is as follows. "Being, but not by way of any becoming; existing, but not from having been nonexistent; with everything, but not through association; and other than everything, but not through separation; acting, but not through movements and instruments; seeing, even when nothing of His creation was to be seen; solitary, even when there was none whose intimacy might be sought or whose absence might be missed."[94]

God is "with everything, but not through association": He is not some separate entity conjoined to the creature, for this would entail a duality — God and the things He is "with"; and "other than everything, but not through separation": His inaccessible transcendence does not imply that He is separate from what He transcends, for this would again entail a duality — God and the things He transcends. Multiplicity is thus integrated within an ontological unity according to Imam ʿAlī's perspective, and this, we believe, is what Eckhart means when he says that "outside God nothing is": the apparent multiplicity of existence is integrated within the true unity of the One — Beyond-Being — in a manner that reflects the way in which the apparent multiplicity of the Trinity is rendered transparent to the unity of its own Essence. To repeat: we should be able "to grasp distinctions without number and quantity," and thereby come to see that Persons or attributes can exist within the Godhead, which nonetheless remains unique and indivisible.

This uniqueness, however, must be conceived as transcending number. Neither threeness nor oneness can adequately describe this one-and-only-ness. Eckhart therefore says that everything uttered about the Trinity "is in no way really so or true . . . because every name or in general every

---

93. See the discussion of this principle, in the context of al-Kāshānī's Sufi commentary on the Qurʾān, in R. Shah-Kazemi, *The Other in the Light of the One: The Universality of the Qurʾan and Interfaith Dialogue* (Cambridge: Islamic Texts Society, 2006), ch. 2, section 1, titled "The One in the Many, the Many in the One," pp. 76-97.

94. Cited in *Justice and Remembrance,* pp. 208-9.

thing that denotes a number, or makes a number come to mind, or be conceived, is far from God." He then quotes a saying from Boethius: "That is truly one in which there is no number."[95]

It is important to repeat here the crucial principle enunciated by Frithjof Schuon, referred to earlier: "Only Unity as such can be a definition of the Absolute; in the realm of number, unity alone represents an element of absoluteness, as does the point or the centre in space, and the instant or the present in time."

The metaphysical perspectives of Eckhart and Ibn al-ʿArabī, St. Dionysius and Imam ʿAlī, help us to perceive the grounds upon which we can affirm unequivocally that Muslims and Christians do believe in the same God. This God can be conceived as That which transcends the domain within which all existential categories subsist, including not just the categories time, space, form, matter, and number, but also all distinct divine attributes. It is thus a Reality which cannot be adequately described, whether by attributes or Persons, for both attributes and Persons are relativities by dint of their very susceptibility to conception in distinct terms, this distinctiveness being an inescapable concomitant of their "ex-istence," taking this word according to its etymological roots, *ex-stare:* their "standing apart from" that all-embracing Reality which cannot be conceived, this inconceivability being the extrinsic, apophatic concomitant of its intrinsic, "superessential" mystery.

3. Contemporary Witness and Philosophical Theology

A Common Word

On October 13, 2007, a groundbreaking interfaith initiative was launched by the Royal Aal al-Bayt Institute in Amman, Jordan.[96] An open letter titled "A Common Word Between Us and You," signed by 138 Muslim leaders and scholars representing every major school of thought in Islam, was sent "to leaders of Christian churches everywhere." This was an invitation to engage in dialogue on the basis of love of God and love of the neighbor, these being recognized as the two "great commandments" enjoined by

---

95. *Meister Eckhart: Teacher and Preacher,* ed. B. McGinn (New York/Mahwah/Toronto: Paulist Press, 1986), pp. 210-11.

96. See www.acommonword.com for the text itself, and the responses thereto.

both traditions. The overwhelmingly positive Christian responses from the leaders of all the major churches implied that the basic, albeit unspoken, premise of the text — belief in the same God — was accepted. Some responses made this more explicit than others. For example, in the response of the Yale Divinity School, we read: "We applaud that *A Common Word Between Us and You* stresses so insistently the unique devotion to one God, indeed the love of God, as the primary duty of every believer."[97]

In his response, the Archbishop of Canterbury, Dr. Rowan Williams, not only affirms that Christians and Muslims believe in the same God, but also goes to great pains to point out that the Trinitarian God is in essence not other than the One God believed in and worshiped by Muslims, even going so far as to apply — whether consciously or not — two Muslim "names" of *Allāh* to the Trinitarian God, that is, *al-Hayy* (the Living) and *al-Qayyūm* (the Self-subsistent). The meaning of the word "God," according to the Archbishop, is "a nature or essence — eternal and self-sufficient life . . . we speak of 'Father, Son and Holy Spirit,' but we do not mean one God with two beings alongside him, or three gods of limited power. So there is indeed one God, the Living and Self-subsistent, associated with no other."[98]

Such explicit affirmation of the identity — the sameness — of the Christian and Islamic God is by no means restricted to our times. The following are some of the noteworthy precedents in the history of Christian-Muslim dialogue:

1. Timothy I (d. 823), Catholicos and Patriarch of the Church of the East, who lived most of his life in Baghdad, center of the Abbasid empire, was summoned to the court of the Caliph al-Mahdī (r. 775-785) to respond to various questions. He asserted clearly his belief that the Prophet Muhammad called people to the one true God:

> Muhammad deserves the praise of all reasonable men because his walk was on the way of the Prophets and of the lovers of God. Whereas the rest of the Prophets taught about the oneness of God, Muhammad also taught about it. So, he too walked on the way of the Prophets. Then, just as all the Prophets moved people away from evil and sin, and drew them to what is right and virtuous, so also did Muhammad move the

97. See, for the full text, "A Christian Response to A Common Word Between Us and You," *New York Times,* November 18, 2007.

98. See the full text of the Archbishop's response on www.acommonword.com.

sons of his community away from evil and draw them to what is right and virtuous. Therefore, he too walked on the way of the Prophets.[99]

2. Pope Gregory wrote to the Muslim King Anzir of Mauritania in 1076, expressing gratitude for a charitable act performed by the latter: "We believe and confess one God, although in different ways, and praise and worship Him daily as the Creator of all ages and the ruler of this world. For as the apostle says: 'He is our peace who has made us both one' (Eph. 2.14)."[100]

3. Pope Pius XI said, when dispatching his Apostolic Delegate to Libya in 1934: "Do not think you are going among infidels. Muslims attain to salvation. The ways of Providence are infinite."[101] If Muslims are not "infidels" they must be included in the category of "believers" — those who believe in the one and only God.

4. Similarly, some two decades later, Pope Pius XII (d. 1959) declared: "How consoling it is for me to know that, all over the world, millions of people, five times a day, bow down before God."[102] Muslims, then, worship the one and only God, the God worshiped by Christians.

Let us now return to the question posed at the beginning of this essay about the degree to which the Trinity is central and indispensable to Christian belief, and ask: What do such affirmations by Christian authorities imply for the status of the doctrine of the Trinity in Christian belief? Three implications might be posited here:

99. Sidney Griffith, *The Church in the Shadow of the Mosque — Christians and Muslims in the World of Islam* (Princeton and Oxford: Princeton University Press, 2008), pp. 104-5. Timothy's statement is all the more remarkable given his refusal to explicitly acknowledge that the Qur'ān was indeed a divine revelation. He believed nonetheless in the sincerity of the Prophet's summons to believe in the one true God and to lead a life of virtue in consequence thereof.

100. See J. Neuner and J. Dupuis, *The Christian Faith in the Doctrinal Documents of the Catholic Church* (London: Collins Liturgical Publications, 1983), pp. 276-77.

101. *L'Ultima* (Florence), Anno VIII, 1934; cited in William Stoddart, *What Do the Religions Say about Each Other? Christian Attitudes to Islam, Islamic Attitudes to Christianity* (San Rafael, CA: Sophia Perennis, 2008), p. 12.

102. Cited in Stoddart, *What Do the Religions Say about Each Other?* p. 12. Abundant material of a similar nature can be found in this valuable compilation of William Stoddart. One should also note here such statements as the following: Pope John Paul II said to a group of Moroccan Muslims (August 19, 1985): "We believe in the same God, the one God, the living God, the God who created the world and brings his creatures to their perfection." For this and other similar statements by modern popes, see http://www.usccb.org/seia/textsislam.shtml.

(1) The doctrine of the Trinity is not an essential element in the Christian belief in one God. That is why we can embrace Muslims as fellow-believers in the one God even if they do not believe in — and indeed, repudiate — the Trinity.

(2) The doctrine of the Trinity is essential to Christian belief in God, and it accurately defines the true, objective nature of that one God; so Muslims who truly believe in the one true God cannot but believe in the Trinity, objectively and in reality, even if they are unaware of the fact subjectively, and fail to register it dogmatically. The task for the Christian here is to say to the Muslims what St. Paul said to the Athenians: "Whom therefore ye ignorantly worship, Him declare I unto you" (Acts 17:23).[103]

(3) The Trinity is essential to Christian belief, but it is possible to conceptually abstract this aspect of belief, and still retain an adequate conception of the Essence of God, the Essence of that divinity believed in and worshiped by Muslims. So Muslims may not believe in the Trinity, but insofar as they believe in God's unicity and simplicity, transcendence and perfection — together with most if not all of the other attributes ascribed to the divine Essence by Christians — they believe in the selfsame Essence or nature of God as posited and articulated in Christian faith.

We have seen in the previous section how Eckhart provides us with grounds upon which this latter position, (3), might be metaphysically articulated. The One, the Ground, the Godhead is "beyond Being," while the Persons of the Trinity are "suspended" at the level of Being, there where God is definable as God in relation to creatures. It was also seen that this corresponds closely with Ibn al-ʿArabī's distinction between two degrees of oneness within the divinity: the oneness of the One, and the oneness of the many. In both cases, plurality within divinity is affirmed without detriment to the unity, simplicity, or transcendence of God, such plurality being situated upon an ontological level transcended by the One, the pure

103. A variation on this position is given by such figures as Abelard and Bonaventure. Abelard affirmed that no Jew or Gentile — nor any person with "common sense" — could doubt that "God is Power, Wisdom and Goodness." Gilles Emory, *Trinity in Aquinas* (Ypsilanti, MI: Sapientia Press, 2003), p. 8. Similarly, Bonaventure gave a host of "natural reasons" proving that God was a Trinity. *Trinity in Aquinas*, pp. 19-20. As we shall see shortly, Aquinas strongly rejects this position: belief in the Trinity requires a leap of faith, and is by no means a logical or natural concomitant of belief in the oneness of God.

Essence. However, one might ask: Is there a way of articulating this perspective in theological terms, doing so by reference to authorities within the Christian tradition who are less controversial than Eckhart? We believe that there is, and this essay will be concluded with a necessarily brief attempt to sketch out such a perspective, doing so in relation to the writings of St. Thomas Aquinas.[104]

St. Thomas Aquinas and the Common Ground of Transcendence

After addressing the question of sacred doctrine in general, Aquinas begins his *Summa Theologica* with a treatise on the unity of the divine Essence. There is little, if anything, in this treatise with which a Muslim could disagree. One reads about God's unity, simplicity, indivisibility, together with such fundamental attributes as the divine perfection, wisdom, and goodness; about divine existence being identical to divine essence, together with a host of explanations pertaining to God's necessary existence — nearly all of which could easily have come from the pen of a philosophically minded Muslim theologian in his description of God.[105] As regards the meaning of the word "God," it is important to note that Aquinas assumes that all of those who speak of "God" have in mind an identical signification, the word or concept always indicating an identical referent: "The name God signifies the divine nature, for this name was imposed to signify something existing above all things, the principle of all things, and removed from all things; for those who name God intend to signify all this."[106] The word "God" thus signifies that supreme reality which transcends all things at the same time as being the source of all things.

104. One might also choose such figures as St. Gregory Palamas and St. Maximus the Confessor, within the Orthodox tradition, whose articulation of the concept of the divine Essence would also provide us with strong grounds for asserting commonality, if not identity, with the Muslim conception of the divine Essence.

105. Indeed, the influence of such philosophers as Ibn Sīnā and al-Fārābī (and such mystical theologians as al-Ghazālī) on fundamental themes of Aquinas's ontology, philosophy, and theology has been amply demonstrated by contemporary scholarship. See, for example, A. M. Goichon, *The Philosophy of Avicenna and Its Influence on Medieval Europe* (Delhi: Motilal Banarsidass, 1969).

106. *The Summa Theologica of St. Thomas Aquinas,* trans. Fathers of the English Dominican Province (Westminster, MD: Christian Classics, 1981), vol. 1, p. 68, I.13.8, reply to objection 2.

As regards the unity of God, Aquinas goes to great pains to assert that the one God is not composed of parts, even though it comprises infinite perfections. Although the divine nature or Essence is absolutely one and noncomposite, it is conceived by the intellect in inescapably multiple ways. Thus, in the effort to understand something meaningful about the nature of God, the human intellect forms conceptions "proportional to the perfections flowing from God to creatures"; these perfections preexist in God "unitedly and simply," whereas in creatures "they are received, divided and multiplied." To these variegated conceptions of different perfections, however, "there corresponds one altogether simple principle," a principle "imperfectly understood" by the different conceptions.[107]

He continues thus, in his reply to objection 3 in this article: "The perfect unity of God requires that what are manifold and divided in others should exist in Him simply and unitedly. Thus it comes about that He is one in reality, and yet multiple in idea, because our intellect apprehends Him in a manifold manner, as things represent Him." Again, none of this would be objectionable to the Muslim theologian. Indeed, the latter might regard such statements as these to be strong evidence for the subjective nature of the doctrine of the Trinity: it is but a mode of "plurality" subsisting in the mind of the creature, not in the objective reality of the Creator, who is "one in reality" and only "multiple in idea."

In his so-called "shorter" *Summa* (titled *Compendium of Theology*) Aquinas makes even clearer the way in which the unicity of the nature/Essence is rendered mentally compound only by and within the human intellect; and he stresses the need to see through our own creaturely categories in order to grasp God's utter unity and simplicity: "If we saw His essence as it is in itself, a multiplicity of names would not be required; our idea of it would be simple, just as His essence is simple. This vision we hope for in the day of our glory; for, according to Zechariah 14:9, 'In that day there shall be one Lord; and His name shall be one.'"[108]

Again, this sounds very much like Islamic *Tawḥīd*. Indeed, Aquinas sums up this part of the discussion dealing with the nature of God by writing: "The truths about God thus far proposed have been subtly discussed by a number of pagan philosophers," by whom he means both Greeks and Muslims. However, when discussion turns to the Trinity, there is an abrupt change of tone:

107. *Summa Theologica*, vol. 1, p. 63, I.13.4.
108. *Aquinas's Shorter Summa*, ch. 24, p. 26.

But there are other truths about God revealed to us in the teaching of the Christian religion, which were beyond the reach of the philosophers. These are truths about which we are instructed, in accord with the norm of Christian faith, in a way that transcends human perception. The teaching is that although God is one and simple, as has been explained above, God is Father, God is Son, and God is Holy Spirit. And these are not three gods, but are one God.[109]

While "pagan philosophers" might well understand such "essential attributes" as divine goodness and wisdom, they cannot grasp the personal properties of the essence, such as paternity and filiation[110] — nor can the Christian prove the existence of such properties by means of the intellect. Aquinas quotes Hilary's statement, from the treatise on the Trinity: "Let no man think to reach the sacred mystery of generation by his own mind"; and Ambrose: "It is impossible to know the secret of generation. The mind fails, the voice is silent." He then adds: "Since, therefore, man cannot know, and with his understanding grasp that for which no necessary reason can be given, it follows that the trinity of persons cannot be known by reason."

He goes so far as to say that any attempt to prove the Trinity by means of reason "derogates from faith," and this in two ways. "Firstly as regards the dignity of the faith itself, which consists in its being concerned with invisible things that exceed human reason." In other words, belief in the Trinity does not derive from anything that reason can deduce from its conception of the divine Essence; rather, it comes exclusively from faith in the specifically Christian revelation, transmitted by authority, and received in a spirit of humble obedience by the faithful soul of the Christian believer. Those things that "exceed human reason" cannot be proven by human reason. Faith is the only means by which these things can be understood: *credo ut intelligam* — "I believe in order to understand," as St. Anselm's famous dictum has it.

The second way in which the attempt to rationally prove the Trinity derogates from faith concerns the question of "drawing others to the faith." He writes:

For when anyone in the endeavour to prove the faith brings forward reasons which are not cogent, he falls under the ridicule of the unbe-

109. *Aquinas's Shorter Summa*, ch. 36, p. 35.
110. *Summa Theologica*, vol. 4, p. 2040, III.3.3.

lievers: since they suppose that we stand upon such reasons, and that we believe on such grounds. Therefore we must not attempt to prove what is of faith except by authority alone, to those who receive the authority; while as regards others, it suffices to prove that what faith teaches is not impossible.[111]

The necessity of the Trinity, then, cannot be demonstrated by reason. There are no arguments that carry sufficient weight to prove the Trinity, but the doctrine might be shown by reason to be "not impossible." In terms of intellectual exposition, then, this is a modest claim: the Christian cannot prove the logical necessity of the Trinity in the way he *can* prove the necessity of the divine Essence. He can at most demonstrate that the Trinity is "not impossible." This means that while non-Christians can never be taught by reason to believe in the Trinity, they might come to see that it is "not impossible" that the essential attributes they can logically deduce from the existence of the Essence might be brought into some kind of correspondence with, or approximation to, the properties of the Persons. Hence:

> The philosophers did not know the mystery of the Trinity of the divine Persons by its proper attributes, such as paternity, filiation and procession, according to the Apostle's words, "We speak the wisdom of God which none of the princes of the world" — i.e., the philosophers — "knew" (I Cor. ii.6). Nevertheless, they knew some of the essential attributes appropriated to the Persons, as power to the Father, wisdom to the Son, goodness to the Holy Ghost.[112]

Here one can see a theological bridge connecting the two traditions. Aquinas accepts that "philosophers," i.e., Muslims and Greeks, can attain knowledge of such essential attributes as power, wisdom, and goodness, attributes that are undifferentiated in the simplicity of the divine Essence, in one respect, while also pertaining, in another respect, to the Father, Son, and Spirit, respectively. It is thus possible for theologians of both traditions to come together on this transcendent common ground constituted by the unicity and simplicity of the Essence, within which certain "essential attributes" are present but undifferentiated. On the basis of this com-

111. *Summa Theologica*, vol. 1, p. 169, I.32.1.
112. *Summa Theologica*, vol. 1, p. 169, I.32.1, reply to objection 1.

mon conception of the transcendent Essence they can affirm: we as Christians and Muslims do believe in the same God, the same God conceived *essentially*. But as regards the appropriation of the essential attributes by the Persons, or the ascription to each of the three Persons of all of the essential attributes, there will be theological disagreement. Nonetheless, the agreement on the plane of the Essence can prevail over disagreement on the plane of the Persons: this may be put forward as the theological premise implicit in the affirmation by Christian theologians — including the Archbishop of Canterbury, and various popes, past and present — that they and Muslims do believe in the same God.

This argument is reinforced when we ask St. Thomas about the formal status of a belief in God that is devoid of any conception of the Christian Trinity. For the answer given by him is as follows:

> If we mentally exclude the personal properties there will still remain in our thought the divine Nature as subsisting and as a Person. . . . Even if the personal properties of the three Persons are abstracted by our mind, nevertheless there will remain in our thoughts the one Personality of God, as the Jews consider.[113]

So even if, like the Jews, Muslims do not believe in the Trinity, what they do believe in — the "divine Nature," the unique "Person," the "One Personality" — is identical to what Christians believe in at that same level of divinity — the transcendent unicity of the divine Essence. This one God is the God of Abraham and Moses, neither of whom made any mention whatsoever of the Trinity, and yet it is affirmed in Christian dogma that it was "the Trinity" who bestowed revelation upon them both, and upon all prophets of God. In the words of the text of the Fourth Lateran Council (1215): "This holy Trinity, which is undivided according to its common essence but distinct according to the properties of its persons, gave the teaching of salvation to the human race through Moses and the holy prophets and his other servants, according to the most appropriate disposition of the times."[114]

---

113. *Summa Theologica*, vol. 4, p. 2040, III.3, a.3, reply to objections 1 and 2.

114. We have taken this translation from the compendium of Catholic documents made available at http://www.documentacatholicaomnia.eu/03d/1215-1215,_Concilium _Lateranum_IIII,_Documenta_Omnia,_EN.pdf. See also Neuner and Dupuis, *The Christian Faith in the Doctrinal Documents of the Catholic Church,* for this and many of the most important doctrinal texts of the Catholic Church.

The Trinity, being "undivided according to its common essence," is thus nothing other than the One God of Abraham and Moses — and of Muhammad, one should add. However, neither Abraham nor Moses nor Muhammad would recognize that this One God is "distinct according to the properties of its persons"; they would not affirm any Trinity within the Unity. So we return to the point just made: Christians do believe in the same God as the Jews and the Muslims — the same God conceived *essentially;* but in addition to this essential belief, Christians also affirm belief in a triune aspect of God, an aspect vehemently denied by Jews and Muslims. One notices here a difference between implication and predication: for Christians, belief in God may well theologically *imply* belief in the Trinity, but is not essentially *predicated* upon it, failing which they could not affirm that Jews and Muslims believe in and worship the one true God. It would appear that the Christian can believe in God, therefore, without this belief being predicated on the Trinity; but the Christian cannot believe in the Trinity without believing in God. This shows that belief in one God — the basic postulate of monotheism — must have primacy over belief in the Trinity. To cite one of the key principles of Thomistic theology: what is common takes priority over what is proper: "What is essential is prior according to our understanding to what is notional, just as what is common to what is proper."[115] What is common to the Persons — the divine nature, substance, or essence — precedes, or takes priority over, what is proper to the Persons — their specific, personal properties; likewise, what is essential or universal in our knowledge takes priority over what is notional or specific. This principle can be applied to the question at issue here: what is common to the two theologies of Islam and Christianity — belief in the one divine Essence — takes priority over what differentiates them — the distinctive "properties" (whether attributes or Persons) ascribed to that Essence within the two theologies.

It is the common ground of affirmation of belief in God as such — God *qua* Essence, Substance, or Nature — that, even in the absence of any reference to the Trinity, allows Christians to affirm that Muslims believe in the one true God, the God of Abraham and Moses. This appears to us logically implied in the statement of St. Thomas: If the Personal properties are abstracted from our minds, "there will still remain in our thought the divine Nature . . . the one Personality of God, as the Jews consider." The

---

115. This is cited from St. Thomas's commentary on Peter Lombard's *Sentences* (I, Sent., d.29, q.1, a.2), in Emory, *Trinity in Aquinas*, p. 179.

Christian conception of God, then, is not undermined by the mental abstraction of the Trinity therefrom: it may be devoid of the plenitude rendered spiritually accessible by explicit recognition of the Trinitarian dimensions of the one God, but it remains nonetheless an adequate doctrinal expression of the one true God postulated by all monotheistic traditions. The Christian theologian might regard the relationship between this kind of unitary conception of God and the full-blooded Trinitarian conception of God as being analogous to the relationship between, on the one hand, an abstract, purely mental conception of a circle, which, being only a conception in the mind, is devoid of any objective dimensions in space; and, on the other, a concrete perception of an actual sphere existing in space. The Christian can then argue *both* that the Muslim/Jewish conception of God is identical to the Christian conception of God — both posit the same conceptual "circle"; *and* that the Christian goes one step further, by grasping the dimensions that are missing from that conception — the concrete manifestation of the abstract circle as an actual sphere. The shift from the one to the other might be seen as symbolizing the shift from transcendence to immanence, or simply: the act by which God becomes incarnate in Jesus — the focal point of theological incompatibility between the two traditions. The Trinity both anticipates and results from the mystery of the incarnation, and for this reason ought to remain bracketed out of any effort to establish common theological ground between the two traditions, this common ground being constituted by the affirmation of the absolute transcendence of the one and only divinity.

Aquinas — and with him, the entire scholastic tradition, it seems — regards the shift from the oneness of God to the Trinity as being a shift from general "metaphysics"[116] to specific "theology."[117] The threeness of God is a greater mystery — greater in the sense of more fully transcendent vis-à-vis the creaturely categories of thought and being — than is the merely metaphysical or philosophical oneness of God. This oneness is something that both the Jews and the Greeks understood. The threeness of

116. We would prefer to call it ontology or philosophy, reserving metaphysics for such perspectives as those of Eckhart and Ibn al-ʿArabī, perspectives that reveal the limitations of theology; see footnote 2.

117. See for example St. Bonaventure's treatise "The Soul's Journey into God," where the final three chapters address, in clearly ascending hierarchical order, the unity of God, the Trinity, and then the flight into "spiritual and mystical ecstasy." *Bonaventure: The Soul's Journey into God, The Tree of Life, The Life of St Francis*, trans. and ed. Ewert Cousins (Mahwah, NJ: Paulist Press, 1978), pp. 94-116.

God, however, spiritually trumps this abstract conception; it more adequately reveals the intrinsic incapacity of human thought to attain knowledge of the mystery of God: "the foolishness of God is wiser than men" (1 Cor. 1:25); it also effectively foreshadows the doctrine of salvation through the cross, which is "unto the Jews a stumbling block, and unto the Greeks foolishness" (1 Cor. 1:23).[118] All three mysteries — Trinity, Incarnation, and the Redemption wrought through the Crucifixion — are summed up in the challenging enunciation by Vladimir Lossky, cited earlier: "The dogma of the Trinity is a cross for human ways of thought."

So the Christian theologian can place Muslims in the same category as the Jews: as St. Irenaeus said, insofar as the Jews believe in God, love Him, and practice virtue, they "reveal one and the same God."[119] Through his detailed elaboration of the doctrine pertaining to the unique nature/Essence of God, then, Aquinas helps to render explicit what is implied in such statements by Irenaeus about the Jews, and those made by the authorities cited above about Muslims: this unique Essence is the common ground upon which all monotheists can come together and assert with unanimity that they believe in the same God. Let us also note that Aquinas's statement that it is possible to abstract the Trinity from one's conception of God, without ruining one's conception of this Essence, is implied in the following declaration of the Fourth Lateran Council. After stating the position of Joachim, who rejected that of Peter Lombard, the following statement is made:

> We, however, with the approval of this sacred and universal council, believe and confess with Peter Lombard that there exists a certain supreme reality, incomprehensible and ineffable . . . each of the three Persons is that reality — that is to say substance, essence or divine nature — which alone is the principle of all things, besides which no other principle can be found. This reality neither begets nor is begot-

---

118. St. Gregory of Nyssa writes that the Christian faith is distinct both from the monotheism of the Jews and the polytheism of the Greeks, a point of view that is summed up by St. John of Damascus, who writes in his *De Fide Orthodoxa* (I, 7): "On the one hand, of the Jewish idea we have the unity of God's nature and, on the other, of the Greek, we have the distinction of hypostases — and that only." Cited by Wolfson, *The Philosophy of the Church Fathers*, p. 363.

119. Even if he also asserts that only through the Son can the Jews be liberated from slavery to God and become friends of God. See *Five Books of S. Irenaeus Against Heresies*, book 4, ch. 13, 4.

ten nor proceeds; the Father begets, the Son is begotten and the holy Spirit proceeds.[120]

Alongside the dogmatic affirmation of the identity of each of the three Persons with the Essence, there is a reference to that Essence in terms that clearly indicate the possibility of distinguishing It from the Persons, and thus, inversely, the possibility of abstracting the Persons from the Essence without detriment to one's conception of the intrinsic nature of the Essence; this essential nature being defined in this conciliar text by the fact that it "neither begets nor is begotten nor proceeds." We are reminded here of Eckhart's statement, cited above: for God to see inside the One "would cost Him all His divine names and personal properties"; only insofar as God is one and indivisible, "neither Father, Son nor Holy Ghost," can He see or enter into the Oneness that Eckhart has discovered. As he said, when defending himself against the accusations of heresy: "Although in God the Father essence and paternity are the same, He does not generate [the Son] insofar as he is essence, but insofar as He is Father, even though the essence is the root of the generation."[121]

It is debatable whether Aquinas would have accepted the implication that Eckhart draws from the fact that the Essence is the "root" of the "generation," namely, that the Essence transcends the Trinity, according to the same principle by which Godhead transcends God, Beyond-Being transcends Being, every cause ontologically precedes its effect, or as the root has priority over the tree. But one can argue nonetheless that for Aquinas the unity of the divine Essence is the philosophical "infrastructure" of the dogma of the Trinity: one has to understand first what the essence or nature of God is, and on this basis proceed to discussion of God qua Trinity. And this indeed is why the *Summa* starts with a treatise on the unity of God and then proceeds to the Trinity.[122] This, together with the fact that he accepts that the unitarian conception of God remains valid on its own level, even if the Trinitarian conception be abstracted from it, means that it

---

120. From the website cited above: http://www.documentacatholicaomnia.eu/03d/1215-1215,_Concilium_Lateranum_IIII,_Documenta_Omnia,_EN.pdf.

121. Cited by Turner, *The Darkness of God,* p. 154.

122. This is the basic argument of Rudi te Velde: "The treatment of the Trinity presupposes therefore a prior clarification of God's activity, which in turn presupposes a clarification of the divine essence (or substance), since the activity follows upon the being of the subject of activity *(agere sequitur esse)." Aquinas on God: The "Divine Science" of the* Summa Theologiae (Aldershot, UK: Ashgate, 2006), p. 69.

is entirely legitimate for Christians to invoke Aquinas's perspectives outlined here as justification for positing the unique Essence of God as that in which Christians, Muslims, and Jews believe, irrespective of the fact that both Muslims and Jews disbelieve in the Trinity.

From the Muslim point of view, the Christian conception of a transcendent Essence which "neither begets nor is begotten[123] nor proceeds," in the words of the Fourth Lateran Council, can form the basis upon which the affirmation can be made that Christians and Muslims do indeed believe in the same God; but, added to this affirmation will come a rejection of the very doctrines — the Trinity and the Incarnation — which the Christians deem to be the ultimate fulfillment of monotheism. And herein lies the core of the mutual theological irreducibility between the two traditions; however, this incompatibility can be accepted on one level, without compromising the compatibility achieved at another: each can recognize the other as a fellow-believer in the one true God. In other words, there can be agreement as regards the fact that God is one and transcends all things, and disagreement over the claim that God is also three and is uniquely immanent in Jesus Christ. But the agreement can take priority over the disagreement, for the agreement is situated on the universal ground of monotheism, and in relation to the transcendent Essence of the one God which defines the very terms of that monotheism; whereas the disagreement is situated on the particular ground of Christian theology, and in relation to the Persons of a Trinity which can be abstracted from belief in God, without this abstraction negating or undermining the essential postulate of monotheism: belief in one God.

Affirming this common ground of transcendence is precisely what Frithjof Schuon calls for: he stresses the need for "spiritual solidarity" between all those "who traditionally take cognizance of transcendence and immortality."[124] As regards the question posed here, Muslims and Christians certainly believe in "transcendence"; they will agree that God is abso-

123. One is reminded here of the fundamental verses of the chapter of sincerity/purity (112): "Say: God is One; God, the Eternally subsistent. He begetteth not, nor is begotten, and there is nothing comparable to Him."

124. Schuon makes it clear that he does not believe it possible or desirable to establish "a generalized metaphysical or quintessential understanding," a project he regards as "self-defeating in practice"; rather, what he has in view is simply the possibility of "an adequate understanding" for the sake of upholding the quintessence of the spiritual heritage of mankind, summed up in the principles of the transcendence of the Absolute, and the immortality of the soul. Schuon, *Logic and Transcendence*, p. 5.

lutely transcendent, but will disagree about how this transcendent divinity relates to and is present within, the created world; that is to say, they will disagree about the modalities of divine immanence, as has been stressed repeatedly in this essay. It is thus significant that Schuon does not talk about immanence in this context of "spiritual solidarity" between believers of different traditions. For the stress on transcendence, by contrast, allows one to build a bridge of unanimity, not just between the theologies of Islam and Christianity, but also between all the great religious traditions of the world. As regards immanence, it is only on the esoteric plane that the two traditions might be seen to be in harmony, but even on this plane there are significant differences as regards spiritual accentuation.[125]

But, returning to transcendence, both traditions are at one as regards all the key features of the essential nature of God, defined above by St. Thomas as "something existing above all things, the principle of all things, and removed from all things." We have seen that, metaphysically, this common belief is rendered irrefutably self-evident, whereas theologically it has all too often been obscured behind impenetrable veils of conflicting linguistic formulations. With the help of St. Thomas, though, we can frame this common belief in terms of philosophical theology — something, that is to say, halfway between theology and metaphysics — focusing on the transcendent common ground, the unique Essence of God, and legitimately bracket out the doctrine of the Trinity for the purposes of affirming belief in that unique Essence.

This abstraction of the Trinity from the Christian conception of God, for the purposes of affirming solidarity with fellow-monotheists, by no means implies any derogation of the Trinity by Christians. On the contrary, it serves to deepen the mystery of the Trinity by denying that it can in any way be brought within the purview of "ordinary" monotheism: the Trinity is an extraordinary instance of monotheism, one that spurns all purely natural reasoning, and calls out to be grasped by the supernatural means proper to specifically Christian faith. As we have seen above, this is what St. Thomas insists upon; anything short of this — any attempt to demonstrate or prove the reality of the Trinity "derogates from faith." Moreover, and surprising as it may seem, this very right to grant Trinitarian dogma a divine right of exemption from the rules of logic, and all merely "natural" modes of reason, can serve both the

---

125. See our forthcoming essay, "Light upon Light? The Qur'ān and the Gospel of St John."

Christian and the Muslim theologian in their effort to embrace each other as fellow-believers.[126]

For the Christian can claim that nothing essential about the Trinity is sacrificed in this embrace: in affirming with Muslims a common belief in the transcendent unity of God, one is affirming belief in one aspect of the doctrine of the Trinity — the rationally demonstrable unity of the common nature shared by the three Persons; while at the same time keeping intact the specifically Christian mystery proper to the other aspect of the Trinity — the fact that it is beyond all rational demonstration, or rather that its divine "logic" only becomes apparent through plumbing the mysteries of contemplative faith. For his part, the Muslim theologian can likewise affirm with Christians a common belief in the transcendent unity of God, without this affirmation in any way implying acceptance of the Trinity: what for Christians is beyond all rational demonstration is for Muslims simply illogical.

In this way, the theologians of both traditions can exercise their right — so crucial to the definition of the theologian *per se* — to bear witness to their faith, doing so in the very bosom of their brotherly embrace as fellow believers. As noted above, the Christian can quote St. Paul's declaration to the Athenians: "Whom therefore ye ignorantly worship, Him declare I unto you." The Christian invitation to the Muslims might be envisaged as follows: we not only believe in the one, transcendent God as you do, but, in addition, we believe that this very God became man without sacrificing any of His transcendence; and that the miraculous nature of this incarnation, once it is accepted and empowered by faith, will allow you to see that the Trinity is in fact the least inadequate expression of the full plenitude, profound mystery, and salvific power of the divine nature.

For his part, the Muslim theologian can embrace Christians as fellow-monotheists, while inviting them to consider the crystalline consummation of the defining principle of the monotheism they share in common: *lā ilāha illa'Llāh*, "no divinity but God," such as it is expressed in

126. What Schuon says about "true ecumenism" is pertinent here: "Either it involves an understanding between the religions which is based upon their common interests in the face of a danger that threatens them all, or it may call into play the wisdom that can discern the one sole truth under the veil of different forms." *Logic and Transcendence*, p. 182. In this final section of the essay we have focused on the "common interests" of all believers in the face of the dangers posed by atheism; whereas in section two of the essay, our concern was with the "wisdom which discerns the sole truth under the veil of different forms."

a myriad of ways by God's ultimate revelation to man, the Glorious Qur'ān. Once it is accepted that the Qur'ān completes the cycle of prophetic revelation, and thereby — uniquely among world scriptures — confirms the validity of *all* previous revelations of God, and *all* previous Prophets; and that it restores not just the pristine purity of the faith of Abraham, but also the primordial nature of man as such *(al-fitra)*, doing so through an all-embracing "law and a way" providentially adapted to meet both the particular needs of man in this last phase of the cycle of humanity and the universal needs of all human cultures until the end of this phase — when this is accepted, then it is entirely logical to take the next step: follow in the footsteps of the last Messenger who was sent by God as the "seal of the Prophets," he who embodied to perfection both the outward clarity and the inner mystery of the Message with which he was charged. In other words, the invitation will be to add to the universal monotheistic principle, expressed by the first testimony, "no divinity but God," the specifically Islamic appeal, not to God become man, but to "the Perfect Man" *(al-Insān al-kāmil)*, this being expressed by the second testimony: "Muhammad is the Messenger of God."

Do We Worship the Same God?

Peter Ochs

"Do we worship the same God?" In what way do I find this question compelling? In this brief essay, I offer what I will call a prayerful response by a Jewish philosopher. I understand this to be a response that integrates as many dimensions of reading and belief as the inquirer is aware of. An alternative I do not pursue is to respond straightforwardly by offering my direct judgments about "the God of Israel" and about the God worshiped by Christians and the God worshiped by Muslims. I am skeptical about our abilities to identify the singularity of each tradition or to speak within a single discourse about all the traditions, however singular or complex each may be. I am not skeptical, however, about the capacities of our traditions to transmit records of divine speech. I therefore find the question "Do we worship the same God?" compelling if it is posed, as it were, to our traditions of transmission rather than to us as individual scholars. The question would then introduce an occasion, as it were, for our listening to a dialogue among these traditions and, only then, as a means of listening to a dialogue among these records of divine speech. I must write "as it were" (כביכול, *k'vyakhol*) since I am writing, after all, as an individual scholar —

My thanks to University of Virginia Ph.D. candidates Peter Kang and Omer Shaukat for contributing to the composition of this essay. Mr. Kang's work extends the Christian postliberalism of Hans Frei and George Lindbeck as well as their critique of supersessionism. Mr. Shaukat's work examines questions of ontology in medieval Muslim and modern Western philosophy.

148

and in the first person no less. There is something counterfactual about the way I am writing this contribution. Yet, invoking comparisons about the one to whom we worship may indeed call for something counterfactual.

1. A Prayerful Response: "I pray that we worship the same God."
The conference question refers to the God whom we worship, rather than the God about whom we offer scholarly claims. This reference is therefore an opening to my entering the discussion without trespassing on my skepticism. I may begin by referring to prayer as the conduit for any measure we may have of the direction of our various prayers. In beginning this way, I understand "worship" as a tradition-specific ritual practice offered, prototypically, in a community of worship and therefore by way of verbalized language (scripturally based) as well as various forms of action. I understand "prayer" as the individual person's practice of offering words to God, separately or in the context of communal worship, and as intimate dialogue or interaction with God. I shall therefore refer to prayer as the practice in relation to which the conference question may be posed: an activity in relation to which the individual scholar qua individual may cognize both the noetic direction of his or her communal worship and any possible measure of different directions of worship. (For the sake of discussion, I refer here to the "direction of worship" as a verbal meeting-place between the rabbinic notion of *kavvanah*, or "intention/direction" of worship, and the phenomenological notions of *noesis* and, specifically, of the *noema* or object of *noesis*.) Phenomenologically, the individual scholar's prayer marks, as well, a region of noetic movement between individuated cognition and participation in worship. The form of this movement will introduce any measure that may be available for comparing one direction of worship and another. Another reason that I invoke prayer is that, if we fail to locate useable measures of this kind, I may at least speak of my *hope* for our sharing a direction of worship, and I think of prayer as an activity through which one offers oneself as willing agent of the One who alone fulfills hopes or does not.

2. A Theopolitical Response: "I believe it is God's will that at this time in our histories we in the Abrahamic traditions declare that we worship the same God, albeit by way of mutually exclusive practices of worship."

This response further contextualizes the prayer I invoked in #1. I assume not only that the direction of worship is measured only within worship but also that any community and tradition's measure of worship may vary from epoch to epoch (and that how epochs are measured is itself a subject of worship). The conference question is therefore situated within a specific epoch of worship (or therefore of what some call "salvation history"). The prayer I offered belongs to this epoch; I do not presume that it applies to any other, short of the end-time.

3. An Eschatological Response: "In the end of days all humanity will worship the one God, Creator of Heaven and Earth. The end-time is present now, was present at creation, and is present all days in the presence of God, in His eternal activity, and in His Word. All who share in His presence do, to the degree of that sharing, live in the end of days. We know that His created and His revealed and redeeming Word directs and instructs us in the ways of living toward His presence; and He has declared His presence with us. But we cannot fully articulate, in our self-conscious means of knowing, how we have and do indeed live in that Presence. We are known by that Presence rather than being individual agents who know that Presence. Therefore, we have reason to expect that the God whom we worship makes Himself present as well in the worship of others. But we cannot say clearly if, when, where, and how He does so — in their worship or, in any exact sense, in our own as well."

This response offers the only means I perceive, thus far, to refer the question "Do we worship the same God?" beyond the context of some prayer within some epoch of worship. It is to refer it to the eschatological end of worship: the direction or noematic referent of such an epoch of worship. Perceived as noema, eschatology offers another object for scholarly study, but in that sense it is also limited to the context of study. One alternative is to refer prayerfully to the eschaton, as I do here. This is to refer to it "vaguely," however, or without the clarity that appears only in individuated cognitions. Another alternative is to observe ways in which the eschaton enters the present moment: within worship, for example, or — in rabbinic terms — in *shabbat*. It remains to be seen, however, if this presence would introduce any manner of cognition and measurement we have not yet already considered.

4. A Rabbinic Response (by which I mean, at once, all of the following: a Jewish-doctrinal response; a response grounded in the literatures and religious authorities of the classical rabbinic sages, as read through the various traditions of commentary they spawned; a halakhic response; an axiologically Jewish response): "There are grounds for a series of competing claims."

a. *There is rabbinic warrant for either affirming or denying that Muslims worship the same God as Jews and that Christians worship the same God as Jews.* (Overall there tends to be more support of Muslim worship than of Christian, except for participants in European Jewish-Christian dialogue.) By way of illustration, I will cite several classical and medieval rabbinic sources.

(1) Some rabbinic thought is quite favorable toward Christian and Muslim belief, including attitudes to non-Jews in general, attitudes to the other Abrahamic religions, and attitudes to Muslims.

There are *generic attitudes to non-Jews:*

For the Rabbis — or at least some of them — Divine prophecy was self-evidently too powerful to be bound by human categories of Jew or non-Jew. While this is not a multi-covenant theology, this strand of Rabbinic thought paves the way for such a possibility: "The prophet Elijah said: I call heaven and earth to bear witness that anyone — Jew or gentile, man or woman, slave or handmaid — if his deeds are worthy, the Divine Spirit will rest upon him" (*Tanna Debai Eliyahu* 9:1). "When the Holy One, Blessed be He, revealed Himself to give the Torah to Israel, He revealed Himself not only to Israel but to all the other nations" (*Sifrei Devarim* 343).[1]

All humanity is beloved by God and chosen from amongst all creation. As Zephaniah has prophesied, the nations will in messianic times all call upon God. The distinction between Israel and the nations is the presence — or absence — of the Sinai revelation. All have the image of God, but the Sinai experience is only for Jews — there are two aspects to our lives. The universal and the particular; the image of God and our commitment to Bible as understood by Rabbinic literature, Torah study, ritual law, and peoplehood.[2]

Next we have examples of *attitudes to the other Abrahamic religions.* The most cited source of favorable attitudes is R. Menaḥem Ha-Me'iri (fourteenth century):

---

1. Alan Brill, "Judaism and Other Religions: An Orthodox Perspective," at http://www.bc.edu/dam/files/research_sites/cjl/texts/cjrelations/resources/articles/Brill.htm.
2. Early modern Italian Bible commentator Obaadiah Seforno, *Light of the Nations,* cited in Brill, "Judaism and Other Religions."

Ha-Me'iri's personal view can best be summarized thus: he held that the exclusion of Christians and Moslems from the category of the idol-atrous — an exclusion which had been suggested purely casuistically by earlier halakhists — was to be acknowledged as a firm and compre-hensive principle. At first sight, the opinion of other halakhists and that of Ha-Me'iri might be taken as identical. Modern scholars, af-fected by an apologetic bias of their own, have read into the Ashkenazi halakhists' views the theory held by Ha-Me'iri.[3]

To take an earlier example, Yehudah Halevi (eleventh century, *Sefer ha-Kuzari*) believed that

all religions that came after the Torah of Moses are part of the process of bringing humanity closer to the essence of Judaism, even though they appear its opposite. The nations serve to introduce and pave the way for the long-awaited messiah. He is the fruit and they, in turn, will all become his fruit when they acknowledge him.[4]

Among modern orthodox commentators of the eighteenth century, Yaakov Emden

stretches the traditional inclusivist position into universal directions: "We should consider Christians and Moslems as instruments for the fulfillment of the prophecy that the knowledge of God will one day spread throughout the earth. Whereas the nations before them wor-shipped idols, denied God's existence, and thus did not recognize God's power or retribution, the rise of Christianity and Islam served to spread among the nations, to the furthest ends of the earth, the knowledge that there is One God who rules the world, who rewards and punishes and reveals Himself to man. Indeed, Christian scholars have not only won acceptance among the nations for the revelation of the Written Torah but have also defended God's Oral Law. For when, in their hostility to the Torah, ruthless persons in their own midst sought to abrogate and uproot the Talmud, others from among them arose to defend it and to repulse the attempts" (*Commentary to Pirke Avot*, 4:13).[5]

3. Jacob Katz, *Exclusiveness and Tolerance: Studies in Jewish-Gentile Relations in Medi-eval and Modern Times* (London: Oxford University Press, 1961), p. 115.

4. Brill, "Judaism and Other Religions."

5. Brill, "Judaism and Other Religions."

Next we consider *attitudes toward Islam.* Medieval Jewish philosophers and mystics who drew on Sufi sources practiced de facto tolerance toward Islam. Examples include Bahya ibn Paquda *(Hovot Halevavot)*, Moses Maimonides *(Moreh Nevikhim)*, Obadyah Maimonides (*Treatise of the Pool, al-Maqala al-hawdiyya)*, Abraham ibn Hasdai (translator of al-Ghazali), and above all Ibn Gabirol (for example, *Ani ha'Ish*). Comparable Muslim influences are evident in *Treatise of the Garden* by Moses ibn Ezra; in Shem Tov ibn Falaquera's *The Book of the Seeker (Sefer ha-Mevaqqesh), Beginning of Science (Reshit hokhmah), Book of Degrees Guide to the Guide (Moreh ha-Moreh);* in Abraham ibn Ezra *(Iggeret Hay ben Meqits);* in Abraham ibn Daud *(Exalted Faith, al-'Aqida al-rafi'a);* in Obadyah b. Abraham b. Moses Maimonides *(Treatise of the Pool, al-Maqala al-hwadiyya).*[6]

(2) Other classical and medieval rabbinic sources were less favorable toward Christian and Muslim belief.

The Talmudic sage Rabbi Johanan says of one who teaches Torah to a non-Jew: "Such a person deserves death [an idiom used to express indignation]. It is like placing an obstacle before the blind" (Sanh. 59a; Ḥag. 13a). And yet if a Gentile studies the Law for the purpose of observing the moral laws of Noah, Rabbi Meïr says he is as good as a high priest, and quotes: "Ye shall therefore keep my statutes, and my judgments, which if a man do, he shall live in them" (Lev. xviii. 5). The text does not specify an Israelite or a Levite or a priest, but simply "a man" — even a Gentile ('Ab. Zarah 26a).[7]

The highly influential medieval commentator Rashi was harsh on those other traditions that sought to uproot Judaism. "His particularism is shown in statements such as: 'I ask from You that Your Shekhinah should not rest anymore on the nations of the world and we will be separate from all other nations' (*Commentary to Exodus* 33:16)."[8] Louis Jacobs adds that, "as a rule, Jewish medieval thinkers considered both Islam and Christianity false religions, while at times exonerating them for the sake of social and economic interaction."[9]

---

6. See, *inter alia,* P. Fenton, "The Arabic and Hebrew Versions of the Theology of Aristotle," in *Pseudo-Aristotle in the Middle Ages: The Theology and Other Texts,* ed. Jill Kraye, William F. Ryan, and Charles B. Schmitt (London: The Warburg Institute, 1986), pp. 241-64; and Ibn Kammuna, *Examination of the Three Faiths,* trans. Moshe Perlmann (Berkeley and Los Angeles: University of California Press, 1971), pp. 148-49.

7. Brill, "Judaism and Other Religions."

8. Brill, "Judaism and Other Religions."

9. Louis Jacobs, "Judaism and Other Religions," in *A Jewish Theology* (New York: Behrman, 1973), pp. 286-87.

Katz cites Rashi's view that Israel's election came after all the other nations rejected God's Torah; Israel thereby gained exclusive access to God's truth (Rashi on Exod. 19:5; Lev. 19:33; Num. 22:5-8). Katz adds that medieval Jewish thinkers tended to identify Christianity with the Talmud's "Rome," that is, an idolatrous nation bent on Israel's destruction.[10] In their debates with Christian polemicists, the commentators Rashbam and Josef Bekhor Shor argued strongly against the divinity of Jesus and the validity of a religion based on belief in the incarnation. For Rabbi Moses of Coucy (in *Sefer Mitsvoth Hagadol*), the Holy One shared His intimate Word only with Israel. Among halakhic sources critical of the other Abrahamic religions, Katz cites *Sefer Ḥasidim* as characteristic in its efforts to exclude contact with, for example, Christian ceremonies or implements. Katz notes how Rabbi Judah He-Ḥasid, like Rabbi Moses of Coucy, went "beyond the Talmud in regulating relations with Gentiles, especially in the field of ethics."[11]

Brill notes that

> The Maharal, Yehudah ben Betzalel Loewe (c. 1525-1609) was an eclectic Renaissance Jewish thinker who served as rabbi in Posen and Prague. His system, like many others in the early modern era, Jewish and non-Jewish, worked by creating binary pairs: in this case the redeemed world's sustaining Jews and their opponents the gentiles. Maharal built his theology more on Midrash with its apocalyptic and typological themes than on Biblical or philosophic universalism. The ancient struggles of Israel with the seven wicked nations and Amalek are ever with us: "Israel and Edom are inverse and opposite — when one is in ascent then the other is in descent" (BT *Sanhedrin* 21b). "At the beginning, Israel is connected to the nations like a shell around a fruit. At the end, the fruit is separated from the shell completely and Israel is separated from them" (*Gevurat Hashem* 23).[12]

While the medieval kabbalists drew heavily on Muslim sources, Brill notes that early modern and later kabbalistic writers, including the early Hasidic masters, gave little credence to non-Jewish belief.

> For [Isaac] Luria, the historical situation of exile is a manifestation of the cosmic reality of rupture and evil. The gentiles are not merely the

10. Katz, *Exclusiveness and Tolerance*, pp. 16-17.
11. Katz, *Exclusiveness and Tolerance*, p. 102.
12. Brill, "Judaism and Other Religions."

Other, or the anti-Israel, as in the less metaphysical approaches of Rashi; they are the same stuff as the evil at the beginning of creation. The internal logic of this myth leads to the radical notion — unsupported by classical Jewish texts — that non-Jews have no souls. . . . R. Schneur Zalman of Liady, the founder of the Chabad Hasidic dynasty, clearly states at the beginning of his work Likkute Amarim *(Tanya)* that, as presented in Lurianic writings, gentiles do not have souls.[13]

b. *There is strong rabbinic warrant for identifying some forms of worship, whether by Jews or non-Jews, as idolatrous and, therefore, as offered to gods other than God.* The Talmudic literature is replete with references to the idolatries of the other nations, the Romans in particular (BT *Avodah Zarah* 46a, *Megillah* 25b). Living among "idolaters" — with whom, however, they often entered into successful sociopolitical and economic interaction — medieval rabbinic authorities gradually developed categories for distinguishing these Christian and Muslim neighbors from the idolaters known by the biblical sources and the rabbinic sages. Katz notes that, for example, in the tenth century, Rabbenu Gershom drew a lesson from Rabbi Yohanan's statement that, while gentiles inside the land of Israel are idolaters, "The gentiles outside the land (of Israel) are not idolaters; they are but continuing the customs of their ancestors" (BT *Ḥullin* 13b). For Gershom, the lesson is that, while gentile Christians outside the land are idolaters in a technical sense, they may be treated as though they were not; Jews in his day may therefore engage in economic relations with neighboring Christians.[14]

c. *There is also strong rabbinic warrant for recognizing that Jews ultimately understand only their own worship and that each religion remains at some point opaque to the other,* as in the position of Rashi cited above.

d. *There is strong rabbinic warrant for recognizing that the God to whom Jews pray makes Himself known in other ways to other peoples (and that means other languages or religious discourses).* This can be seen in the positions of Halevi and Seforno cited above.

e. *I believe that rabbinic doctrine defines the limits within which I can respond to this question. Within those limits, however, it refrains from offering me any one determinate response.* In other words, rabbinic doctrine requires me to make fresh judgments on the basis of the issues and evidence before me at the time of this judgment. Within this essay, my judgment is

---

13. Brill, "Judaism and Other Religions."
14. Katz, *Exclusiveness and Tolerance,* pp. 36-37.

therefore displayed only through the unity of all eight levels of my response (from prayer through philosophy back to prayer).

I am skeptical, in other words, that the conference question would be adequately served by efforts to identify the doctrinal basis, within each tradition, for recognizing and measuring other traditions' directions of worship. These efforts are indeed helpful introductory exercises: enabling participants to verbalize measures, within each worshiping community, for evaluating the directions of worship (my reticent phrase for the noemata of worship and prayer). But these exercises do not clarify for us the character or directions of others' worship. My skepticism reflects my assumption that the God to whom we worship is known only as He knows us, as participants in a worshiping community, so that reflecting on doctrines enables us to see more clearly how He knows us but not necessarily how He knows others. My review of rabbinic doctrine enables me to measure the limits of my participation in the work of the conference. Just as it allows noetic movement between scholarship and communal worship, prayer also discloses the limits of this movement — just how far it will stretch, on the one hand, to meet cognition's demands for clarity and, on the other hand, to honor the locality of communal worship.[15]

5. A Scriptural Response (a response grounded in readings of the Abrahamic scriptural narratives): "The narratives of ancient Israel, as displayed in Tanakh, in the New Testament, and in the Qur'ān, are framed within and extend the terms of the religion of ancient Israel. There is therefore strong narrative warrant for speaking of the Abrahamic religions as sharing a narrative frame for characterizing God's identity as, for example, creator of the universe, revealer of His word and will, commander of human behavior, teacher of ultimate wisdom, author of universal redemption in the time to come, a dear friend and ultimately a lover of those who love Him, the only source of our being, knowledge, and peace. There are also narrative grounds for distinguishing different spheres of God's self-identity as known in these different traditions. But there are at the same time strong narrative warrants for identifying different and at times seemingly mutually exclusive subcommunities *within* these traditions, making competing claims about the divine identities even within these traditions."

---

15. To invoke Hans Frei, "The 'Literal Reading' of Biblical Narrative in the Christian Tradition: Does It Stretch or Will It Break?" in *The Bible and Narrative Tradition*, ed. Frank McConnell (New York: Oxford University Press, 1986), pp. 36-77.

This scriptural response introduces a potential source of movement from rabbinic doctrine toward the setting I will recommend for addressing the conference question: inter-Abrahamic scriptural study (Response #7). This movement begins with the rabbinic practice of prooftexting Tanakh as a warrant *(asmachta)* for innovations in the sages' halakhic and aggadic reasonings and with the rabbinic practice of rereading the written Torah as stimulus to ever-new, context-specific *midrashim,* or performative interpretations. Analyzing rabbinic hermeneutics through the lens of contemporary Jewish philosophy and semiotics, I suggest that the plain sense of Tanakh appears within these rabbinic practices as a plenum of really possible meanings of the divine word: a source of indefinitely renewed readings, each one appropriate to its time and context. When understood in this way, the *peshat* is authoritative but irremediably vague, its meaning and performative force clarified only with respect to such context-specific readings.

6. A Jewish Philosophic Response: "For our day the most significant elements of a Jewish philosophic response are":

a. *Distinguishing levels of reading, beginning with the distinction between plain sense (peshat) and interpreted sense (derash):* I believe this elementary rabbinic distinction makes a significant contribution to our discussion. For the Talmudic authors, *peshat* does not mean what some later medieval commentators took to mean "the literal sense." *Peshat* means the sense or place of a verse or verses in their somewhat broader literary context, such as the meaning of "earth" within the specific plot of Genesis 1. As opposed to literal sense, however, *peshat* does not include the ostensive reference of such a term: in this case what we may imagine "earth" means as some physical part of the universe wholly independent of the biblical narrative. *Peshat* also lacks any performative or what some call "readerly-collusive" meaning: what the verse or verses tell us to do or believe. In the terms of my own favorite semiotic, or theory of signs, I would say, perhaps more starkly, that the *peshat* refers only to a verse's internal sense in the flow of a narrative; by itself it has no determinate meaning for us. I believe that, for the rabbinic sages, such determinate meaning is to be found only in some level of interpretive meaning: through the interpreting community and individual's lived relationship to the verse and to the broader scriptural literature. In the most general sense *derash* refers to any level of interpretive meaning of this kind. I think this is a powerful distinction because it means that God speaks to us by way of the *langue* (in this sense, "the alphabet") of *peshat,* but only as enacted in the *parole* (in this sense, "speech-acts") of those who in a given time and place hear the scriptural word as commanding this or that action and revealing this or that truth. In these terms what do we mean when we name or characterize the one whom we worship? Our utterance has to make sense in itself — it has to have a plain sense — but what is its determinate, interpreted meaning? If we maintain this distinction between sense and meaning, then our discussions about "the same God" will have to be nuanced. We will have disclaimed our capacities to appeal directly through our utterances to some publicly visible clear and distinct entity about which we can say, "Oh yes, it is this not that." It means that outside of the intimacy of any moment of vision or relation our accounts will always bear the modesty we associate with "mediated" or "interpretive" or "context-specific" accounts.[16]

16. Lest readers fear my response in #6a is meant to be relativistic or nominalist, I will add this somewhat more technical addendum for those interested. I mean to suggest that there are different modes of signification, and not every mode is adequate to representing any aspect of the Divine life or our relationship to it. For example, if I speak about "the toaster oven over there," I assume my listener and I share and make appropriate use of two semiotic conventions. The first is to assume that, within the degree of precision needed for our communication, I can predicate certain descriptive terms of something "out there" and I can assume that my listener has a pretty good idea of what I mean by those terms and has an adequate ability to look out there and confirm whether or not he or she would also predicate those terms in the same way. We could call this the convention of shared predications (or agreement about the iconic use of signs). A second convention that we share — call it the conventional rules for ostensive reference — is that I can offer a judgment about something "out there," meaning independent of both my listener and me. The convention implies that when I offer such an utterance I can be reasonably assured that my listener will know *where* "out there" he or she should look to perceive something that will clarify or test what I've just uttered (we could also call this conventional use of indexical signs). In these terms, my response #6a is meant to indicate that neither the iconic nor the indexical conventions nor any combination of them is adequate to deliver information about my relationship to (including worship of) God or any aspect of the Divine life. There are other conventions, however, through which I can indeed make such references. These conventions tend to bear such names as "performative reference," "triadic" or "multidimensional interpretation," or various kinds of reference that are offered only within the context of explicit forms of interactive relations. To give one illustration of the latter, I mean that I cannot adequately point to or characterize the one whom I worship except insofar as my listener shares some previously understood community of religious practice and speech with me; even then many such references may need to bear what some call "indexical markers": that is to say, even for religious compatriots, my references have to signal in various ways the lived context of experience, relation, and speech with respect to which the references I've offered have meaning. I mean to indicate furthermore that these semiotic and epistemological challenges operate within a given Abrahamic tradition as well as across those traditions. I have added that this does not lead me to some utterly apophatic conclusion, but to additional levels of response.

b. *Refining our semiotic or logical tools for discriminating and clarifying the many constituents of interpretive meaning:* I am concerned that, just as modern thought weakened our trust in the disciplines of traditional exegesis, so too the postmodern turn has weakened our trust in the efficacy of disciplined reasoning. I maintain my trust, however, that the discourses of Scripture and of rabbinic interpretation are highly disciplined and that if inspected adequately (or "rubbed" as one rabbinic sage put it[17]), they may display to us the very patterns of self-corrective reasoning — *logoi* or *s'vora* — that we may seek but despair of finding. Not just any way of reasoning about "the same God" will uncover the answers we seek. Having been disciplined by scriptural reading and rabbinic interpretation reasoning, I must, for example, identify this locution — "the same God" — as invoking a finite set of scriptural terms, each of which bears a set of "plain senses." Each plain sense, furthermore, yields its own sizable set of interpreted meanings, each of which invokes its time and place and context in a reading community's salvation history. So, for example, the Jewish worshiper may direct his or her intentionality *(kavvanah)* to Elohim Creator of heaven and earth *(bore olam),* or to "You, *Adonai" (atah hashem),* or "God of Abraham" *(elohei avraham),* or "God of Sarah" *(elohei sarah),* or "the Holy One" *(hakadosh baruch hu)* or to any of the many epithets for the One whom one embraces in the darkness of prayer. And out of what context of communal participation, of personal life, and of the history of Israel does one invoke these epithets? And what of the performative force of the invocation? One may understand "interpreted meaning" to include the meaning's performative force as well. Even within the biblical plain sense, for example, consider the difference between the way Amos invokes the God of Israel who condemns the injustices of Israel's kings and the way Hosea invokes the God of Israel who finds Israel in her blood and soothes her after her suffering. Do these prophets invoke "the same God"? When one refers to "God," does that mean one is referring ostensively to some single object "out there," or, is one invoking an infinite set about which one cannot measure sameness or difference? Or is one invoking that One who, however infinite and inscrutable, gives Himself here and now to the singularity of the relationship that binds this one seeker to this One who also seeks? All these questions come, moreover, even before we entertain the possibility or the prospect of measuring the sameness or difference that link or do not link the one whom this Jew worships to the one whom this Christian worships and this Muslim wor-

---

17. *BT Tractate Shabbat* 38b.

ships. I do not believe these questions are unanswerable — whether wrapped in infinite mystery or disbarred by some logical rule — but I do believe the answers will be nuanced and many-leveled.

c. *But how would we choose a language in which we could pursue such nuanced and many-leveled answers? Is the language generated out of some a priori rules of construction (like an artificial language of science or logic)? Or is it drawn strictly out of revealed sources (scriptures)? Or do we hear it somehow afresh in response to an unexpected question (as unanticipated as revealed Scripture, but also constructed out of what we already know)?* From out of the resources of contemporary Jewish philosophy, the answer I hear to these questions is inexact. I am drawn to classical biblical and rabbinic discourse, in which the primary verb for "knowing God" is *yāda'*: the same term for "knowing" as in "Adam knew Eve" or as in "Before I formed you in the womb I knew you" (Jer. 1:5). This verb does not refer to knowledge at a distance or to knowledge by identity (that we know God only by participating in God). *Yāda'* is knowledge through intimate relationship, and like interpersonal relations it is a relationship that begins in time and develops, moves, changes, grows deeper.

To say that "I worship God" is therefore at the very least to say that I count myself as having some manner of intimate relation with God. Can I talk about the intimate relations I have with friends? Yes, but I would not presume to "capture" those relationships through simple predicative characterizations or simple ostensive references or pointings — as if to say that I could fully describe my wife in a word or even in a very long string of sentences. I would not rely merely on utterances as a means of sharing with someone else any significant aspects of my intimate relation with God. Nor would I be silent or give up on communication. Instead, I would first acknowledge that my relation to God is articulated through patterns of action, cognition, feeling, expectation, and interrelation (the list continues indefinitely) and that I discern in these patterns a more precise register of my knowledge of God than I can articulate — at least outside of my worshiping community — in the sentences of any natural language. To share what I know with someone else, I must therefore enter into a relationship with this person that will, like any other relationship, begin in time, develop slowly, move, change, grow deeper. Within the complex life of that relationship, my interlocutor and I could share familiarity with certain patterns of life and thought, and I could then speak of aspects of my knowledge of God by pointing to, commenting on, or drawing analogies with these patterns. Over time, we two may develop a linguistic shorthand for the ways we tend to refer to these patterns. Within the limits of our constructed vocabularies and shorthand, we may, only then, begin to share some of our knowledge of divine things.

I think this is one of the profound dimensions of Jewish belief and ontology. It is signaled in the famous dicta of Jewish sages, classic and modern: The words of the rabbinic sage Hillel, "If I am not for myself, who will be for me, But if I am for myself alone, what am I?" The words of Martin Buber, "In the beginning was relation." And Emmanuel Levinas's references to "proximity" and to the "face of the other." As for our present conversation about "the same God," I believe this Jewish wisdom leads to the following recommendation: if a Christian or a Jew wants to discuss whether "a Muslim, Christian, or a Jew" does or does not worship the same God, the "Muslim, Christian, or Jewish" interlocutors will first have to enter into significant relations, one with the other with the other. Only by way of a three-part relationship of this kind can meaningful and verifiable claims be offered about the relationship between the God whom I worship and whom you worship. By the standard of Jewish wisdom I have just called upon, this relationship will have to begin somewhere in time and it will take some time to develop, evolve, change, and move until a response to our question can begin.

7. A Scriptural Reasoning Response

There are many ways in which Muslims, Jews, and Christians may interact with one another so that, over time, they could share conditions for articulating significant characteristics of the One to whom they each pray. Scriptural Reasoning (SR) represents one practice of this kind. Nurtured since 1995 by a society of Christian, Muslim, and Jewish scholars, it is a practice of shared scriptural study. The rules of practice are simple: join a small fellowship of study (eight to twenty persons, but subdivided into study groups of no more than six to eight persons); meet regularly (perhaps every two weeks or monthly for two-hour sessions; or every two to three months for four-hour sessions; or twice annually for sessions of two days or more); focus group study on small excerpts from the three Abrahamic scriptures, spending hours on short selections so that there is time for the texts to become windows to each other and to the heart-knowledge-minds of all participants; study as if all participants shared in each scriptural tradition, in the sense of being invited equally to read, question, and explore possible meanings of each word and verse; privilege no individual person or tradition's voice or authority. (Ideally, the traditions' "plain sense" readings of the texts are introduced in their primary languages by those capable of doing so. But, after initial introduction, the English translations are read as if they were traditional, so that all have equal access to the discussion — albeit with openings to alternate translations to "rub" the primary languages' polyvalence.) The "reasoning" of Scriptural Reasoning is what may happen over time as trajectories of discussion and interpretation emerge that do not appear to belong specifically to any one text tradition or (to be sure!) to any one discipline of the academy.

Scriptural Reasoning would, I believe, offer an optimal context for conversing about each tradition's relation to "the same God (or not)." This study would not prepare participants to learn and recognize their several traditions' doctrines about the identities of the one whom other traditions worship. Participants would pursue such study outside the SR circle, each within his or her "own" tradition. (SR folks tend to call such primary study "textual reasoning" — that is, studying according to the interpretive texts that limn each tradition of commentary.) To enter SR study is to come in some sense already settled in the range of one's traditional doctrines: coming now to meet the other more directly and intimately. Over time (it is not a quick practice!) SR study should — in grace — nurture the depth of interpersonal and thus intertraditional relations appropriate to hearing and seeing meaningful aspects of the relations that trace each participant's "knowledge" of the one to whom he or she prays. *Elemental features of this study are: raising the question of others' worship only in the company of those others; and in the context of philosophically disciplined, doctrinally resourced, prayerfully engaged, theopolitically alert, shared study of our different but sometimes overlapping narrative sources and traditions.*

From my perspective as a Jewish philosopher, Scriptural Reasoning introduces the most — or perhaps only — compelling setting for responding to the conference question, since it honors each of the previous responses.

8. A Prayerful Unity of Responses

If, at this time in theohistory, I pray that we worship the same God, I also pray that I take up such a question only in the fullness of my life with God, among the people Israel. Within the terms of this essay, "the fullness of my life" is represented by my capacity, in grace, to attend to and engage equally all eight (or more) dimensions of reading and belief. The integrity of my participation in such a discussion would depend on the integration of all these dimensions as well as on my integration into an appropriate circle of intertraditional, theological study. To achieve this integrity, I have "work" to do — as suggested in this essay — but in the end I can only pray that the work is met by the work of others and by divine favor.

In closing, I summarize the assumptions that underlie the network of the eight responses I have offered to the question "Do we worship the same God?" These responses draw me to the conclusion that the question is compelling only when taken up by something like an inter-Abrahamic fellowship of Scriptural Reasoning:

- Other peoples and other individuals may worship in an idolatrous fashion and, thus, worship someone I do not know or seek to worship the one I know but in a fashion that profoundly obscures His identity.
- I would not, however, make judgments about others' worship until I had extended contact with them. I cannot make *a priori* judgments about what God is doing with and in relation to other peoples, as well as with and in relation to other individuals of the people Israel. Other peoples may profess knowledge of "God," but display something else. Or, they may profess knowledge of some god I do not recognize; but their manner of worship and life may suggest to me an unexpected relation to the God I know. Other Jews, for that matter, may profess doctrinally rabbinic belief in God, but until I enter into relationship with them and see how they eat, sleep, and pray, I would not be able to comment on the object and nature of their worship.
- Traditional rabbinic doctrine sets the parameters for a Jewish philosopher's response to the conference question. But I discover that, on this question, there are rabbinic sources for both affirming and denying that Christians and Muslims worship the same God, creator of heaven and earth. As a consequence, I read rabbinic doctrine, performatively, as sending me out to look and see and hear about the practices of this or that Christian and this or that Muslim before I would be able to offer a reasonable judgment about whose worship may or may not be to the one God.
- There are modern and contemporary rabbinic arguments for or against engaging in the intense relationships with other religionists that, I believe, are a prerequisite to asking this question.[18] Once

18. Of those who argue "for," Alan Brill cites, for example, Rav Abraham Isaac Kook, first Ashkenazi chief rabbi in the modern land of Israel: "As for other religions, in my opin-

again, I read the equivocal voice of Jewish wisdom on this question as a sign that the answer depends on when and where and why I en-

---

ion, it is not the goal of Israel's light to uproot or destroy them, just as we do not aim for the general destruction of the world and all its nations, but rather their correction and elevation, the removal of dross. Then, of themselves, they shall join the Source of Israel" (*Iggrot ha-Rayah* 112); "It is necessary to study all the wisdoms in the world, all ways of life, all different cultures, along with the ethical systems and religions of all nations and languages, so that, with greatness of soul, one will know how to purify them all" (*Arpelei Tohar* 33). Brill also cites "The current Chief Rabbi of England, Rabbi Jonathan Sacks, [who] became embroiled in controversy for stating a similar sentiment in the first edition of his work, *The Dignity of Difference,* writing, 'In the course of history, God has spoken to mankind in many languages: through Judaism to Jews, Christianity to Christians, Islam to Muslims.' He was forced to clarify the statement as, 'As Jews we believe that God has made a covenant with a singular people, but that does not exclude the possibility of other peoples, cultures, and faiths finding their own relationship with God within the shared frame of Noahide law.'"

As for those who argue "against," Brill cites the son of Rav Kook, Zevi Yehudah Kook, whose "ideology makes him the father of the settler movement and therefore influential in late twentieth-century Israeli political life." The fruit of Zevi Yehudah Kook's exclusivist ideology can be seen in the conflict his students have caused and embraced with the Palestinians. The ideology itself is noteworthy for a staunch anti-Christianity that culls two millennia of sources without acknowledging any of the countervailing traditions. For Zevi Yehudah Kook, the attack on Christianity is motivated by the conflict with the wider Western culture that both threatens the Jewish purity of Israel from within and opposes his messianic settlement drive from without. Zevi Yehudah Kook resurrects many of the classic anti-Christian polemics with a vigor not seen for centuries (Zevi Yehudah Kook, *Judaism and Christianity* [in Hebrew] [Beit El, 2001]).

On a much gentler and more respectful level, I would add the teachings of Rav Soloveitchik (often known as "the Rav"), who strongly opposed interreligious dialogue. His namesake, Meir Soloveichik, explains why:

> The Rav's opposition to communal, and organizational interfaith dialogue was partly predicated upon the prediction that in our search for common ground — a shared theological language — Jews and Christians might each sacrifice our insistence on the absolute and exclusive truth of our respective faiths, blurring the deep divide between our respective dogmas. In an essay titled "Confrontation," Rabbi Soloveitchik argued that a community's faith is an intimate, and often incommunicable affair. . . . In his essay, the Rav warned that sacrificing the exclusive nature of religious truth in the name of dialogue would help neither Jews nor Christians. Any "equalization of dogmatic certitudes, and waiving of eschatological claims, spell the end of the vibrant and great faith experiences of any religious community," he wrote.

Meir Soloveichik, "How Soloveitchik Saw Interreligious Dialogue," *The Jewish Daily Forward,* April 15, 2003; available online, http://www.forward.com/articles/8692/, accessed September 1, 2009. The reference is to Joseph B. Soloveitchik, "Confrontation," in *Tradition: A Journal of Orthodox Thought* 6, no. 2 (1964).

tertain it. I judge this to be a theopolitical question that, in this day and age, has become an urgent one.

Recommended Reading

Let me recommend several secondary readings that are easily available and provide fine introductions to the literature on Jewish attitudes toward Christian and Muslim beliefs.

> Alan Brill, "Judaism and Other Religions: An Orthodox Perspective," at http://www.bc.edu/research/cjl/meta-elements/texts/cjrelations/resources/articles/Brill.htm#_ednref8T. Brill's essay cites a full range of classical and medieval rabbinic sources on the other religions. (Dr. Brill also has a forthcoming book on the topic.)
>
> David Novak is always a great help on such things. See for example his books *Jewish-Christian Dialogue: A Jewish Justification* (New York and Oxford: Oxford University Press, 1989); and *The Image of the Non-Jew in Judaism: An Historical and Constructive Study of the Noahide Laws* (Lewiston, NY: Edwin Mellen Press, 1983).
>
> A classic source on Jewish-Christian relations in the late medieval and modern periods is Jacob Katz, *Exclusiveness and Tolerance: Studies in Jewish-Gentile Relations in Medieval and Modern Times* (New York: Behrman House, 1961).
>
> Also helpful is Louis Jacobs, "Judaism and Other Religions," in *A Jewish Theology* (New York: Behrman House, 1973), pp. 284-92. For a more recent work, see Jacob Neusner and Bruce Chilton, *Christianity and Judaism: The Formative Categories,* and *Revelation: The Torah and the Bible* (Philadelphia: Trinity Press International, 1995) and continuations.
>
> On early Jewish attitudes toward Christianity, and Christian attitudes toward Judaism, see, *inter alia,* William Horbury, *Jews and Christians in Contact and Controversy* (Edinburgh: T. & T. Clark, 1998); Jacob Neusner, *Judaism and Christianity in the Age of Constantine* (Chicago and London: University of Chicago Press, 1987); E. P. Sanders, *Paul and Palestinian Judaism* (Minneapolis: Fortress Press, 1987).

Contributors

Alon Goshen-Gottstein, Executive Director, The Elijah Interfaith Institute

Peter Ochs, Edgar M. Bronfman Professor of Modern Judaic Studies, University of Virginia

Amy Plantinga Pauw, Henry P. Mobley Jr. Professor of Doctrinal Theology, Louisville Presbyterian Theological Seminary

Christoph Schwöbel, Professor of Systematic Theology, University of Tübingen

Reza Shah-Kazemi, Research Fellow, The Institute of Ismaili Studies

Denys Turner, Horace Tracy Pitkin Professor of Historical Theology, Yale Divinity School

Miroslav Volf, Henry B. Wright Professor of Systematic Theology, Yale Divinity School